PREACH
ANOTHER
STORY

JOHN E. HUEGEL

PREACH
ANOTHER
STORY

A COLLECTION OF SERMONS IN STORY
FORM FROM THE OLD TESTAMENT

Rev. date: 07/13/2017

CONTENTS

Dedicated to all those who love the stories from the Bible.

INTRODUCTION

In response to my collection of sermons in story form based on the New Testament and published under the title *Preach a Story*, I received the following comment from my dear friend and colleague Sara Dixon: "*Preach a Story* is a hit, a keeper for all time. Wonderful for children, young people, adults and folks like me, a refresher with new insights – one for enjoying the old stories we've heard all our life... This Christian educator recommends it for church libraries, preachers, new Christians, seekers and life-time Christians." These words and the response of people in the churches where I have presented the book have prompted me to attempt a similar collection of sermons in story form based on the Old Testament.

The author of Hebrews starts out his epistle with these words: *In the past God spoke to our ancestors through the prophets at many times and in various ways...* The Old Testament is filled with interesting people, many of whom perceived God speaking to them in amazing ways, under various circumstances, and at different times. I wish to retell some of their stories.

The stories I have chosen fit chronologically into the narrative of Israel's history, beginning with Abraham and concluding with the destruction of the city of Jerusalem, the exile, and the rebuilding of the temple and the city. The promise to Abraham in the first story is reaffirmed to the prophet Zechariah in the closing story:

I will make you into a great nation,
and I will bless you; and all peoples on earth...
will be blessed through you. (Ge 12:2,3)
And many peoples and powerful nations will come to Jerusalem
to seek the Lord Almighty and entreat him... (Zec 8:22)

As in the first book, in many of the stories I impersonate the main characters and try to recreate the situations in which they lived, quote freely from various versions of the Biblical text in the narratives and dialogues, and supply appropriate, though imaginary, details. In some of the other stories, I attempt to see the main character through the eyes of a close associate.

Many expositors have found an inexhaustible mine of moral and ethical instruction in the stories of the Old Testament, but I have chosen to let the stories speak for themselves. Since I believe they have inherent power to move us, I have tried to avoid lessons drawn from the stories and invite my readers to let the stories speak to their particular situations and enrich the stories of their own lives.

St. Paul has written: *For everything that was written in the past was written to teach us, so that through the endurance taught in the Scriptures and the encouragement they provide we might have hope* (Ro 15:4). At first glance, it would seem that Paul suggests using the Old Testament for moral teaching, and this is true. But upon closer observation, we notice that he says that the endurance and encouragement we get from the Old Testament provide us hope. I trust that this second collection of sermons in story form, *Preach Another Story*, may be a source of encouragement and hope to those who read them.

1

SARAH CONFRONTS ABRAHAM

Genesis 12, 16-19, 21, 22

My parents gave me the name Sarai, and my husband's name was Abram. His story is well known, and he has received much recognition because of his faith and obedience. But I would like to tell you our story from my point of view.

We were both born in the city of Ur of the Chaldeans on the banks of the Euphrates River, in the region of Mesopotamia. Ur is a university town, a center of culture and learning. My husband had many possessions, and we were living comfortably, surrounded by our extended family, when my father-in-law, Terah, decided we should move to Canaan, a place I had never heard of. I had mixed feelings about this, not too happy about leaving my father and mother, but I felt excited over the adventure.

After months of traveling west over the desert, we finally got as far as Haran, a town on a small tributary of the Euphrates River, seven hundred miles from Ur. Since it is located on the main trade route between Babylon and the Mediterranean, Terah decided we should settle there.

My husband built up a prospering business in camels and sheep, but after his father died, he grew restless. One time, when he came back from the fields, I could tell from the look on his face something had happened to him.

That evening he took me aside and said, "The Lord spoke to me this morning and told me that we should leave this place and go to a land he will show us. Then he said to me:

> *'I will make you into a great nation,*
> *and I will bless you;*
> *I will make your name great,*
> *and you will be a blessing....*
> *and all peoples on earth*
> *will be blessed through you.'"*
> (Ge 12:2, 3b)

My husband squeezed my hand and said firmly, "I believe we should follow the Lord's instructions."

Oh no, I thought, not another long trip... Then I wondered how in the world we could become a great nation, since I didn't even have any children. I could tell that Abram was convinced this is what we should do. I had been raised to be submissive and obedient to my husband's wishes so I didn't even try to dissuade him.

We gathered the servants, all our possessions and animals, Lot, Abram's nephew with his family, and set off traveling south. Months later we arrived at Shechem where we set up camp under an enormous tree. There the Lord appeared to my husband and told him that this was the land he had promised to give him. My husband built an altar to the Lord there.

During the time we spent wandering around the area trying to find an appropriate place to settle permanently, the rains ceased, the wadis, or watercourses, dried up, many of the animals died, and Abram decided we had to go down to Egypt to find food for our household and the few animals that were left. The situation was desperate, and another long trip was necessary.

When we finally got back to Canaan, we settled in the hill country in a place called Hebron and pitched our tents in the shade of some large oaks. While we had been in Egypt, Abam and Lot had acquired some animals. These animals began to multiply so that the grazing land around Hebron could no longer support both of our flocks and herds. Lot and his family moved and settled in the floodplain of the Jordan River, near the city of Sodom.

One night sometime later, while we were sleeping, my husband suddenly awoke. He told me he had just had a vision in which the Lord had promised to be his shield and great reward. However, in the vision he, Abram, reminded the Lord that since he had no children, his servant Eliezer would inherit all his wealth, and that the greatest reward he could receive would be to have his own son. My husband could not go back to sleep so he got up and went outside.

A little later he came back in and said, "I was out there looking up at the countless stars, amazed and awestruck, when I heard the Lord promising me that my offspring would be as numerous as the stars in the sky. I responded by assuring him that I believed this would be true."

Abram crawled back into bed, hugged me and said confidently, "We are going to have a child."

In the culture in which we live, barrenness is considered a disgrace. My servants and our Canaanite neighbors often ask me what kind of a God we worship who would promise a man a son and then keep his wife from having one. I desperately wanted a son. But as the years went by, I could not conceive. Since my husband firmly believed that the Lord was going to give him a son, I wondered if I should help God along in this matter and decided he should sleep with my Egyptian servant Hagar. Perhaps she could conceive and give him a son. When I suggested this to him, he thought it was a good idea.

Hagar did conceive, and she bore a son Ishmael. Then the problems began. I realized what a serious mistake I had made. She despised me, wanted to be the mistress of the house, and have her son become the rightful heir. I told my husband we had to get rid of Hagar and her son, otherwise they would cause us much trouble.

Sometime later, when God reaffirmed the promise he had made to my husband, the Lord changed his name from Abram to Abraham, *father of many nations*, and mine from Sarai to Sarah, *mother of kings*.

One day, when it was beastly hot, Abraham was sitting in front of our tent trying to cool off. He spotted three men on the side of the road and thought it would be a friendly gesture to invite them to sit under the shade of the tree, take off their sandals, and wash their feet. When you have been walking on the desert sand in the heat of the day, nothing is as refreshing as sitting in the shade of a big tree and dipping your feet in a cool basin of water.

The men accepted the invitation, and then Abraham told them they should stay and get something to eat before they continued on their way. He came into the tent, and I knew right away what he wanted me to do.

He said, "Honey, get three pounds of that special flour and bake some of those delicious biscuits, I so enjoy, for these three men."

He ran out and selected a tender calf from the fold and told his servant Eliezer to get the fire ready in the big earthen oven and prepare the meat. After I had finished kneading the flour, I put it in the oven, along with the meat, and soon we had the meal ready. The men dove in as only hungry travelers can, and the conversation picked up.

I was standing behind the flap, just inside the tent, when I heard the men ask, "Where is your wife?"

Abraham responded, "There in the tent."

Then I heard one of them say, "I will surely return to you about this time next year and your wife will have a son."

I couldn't contain myself and burst out laughing. A question danced around in my head, will I really have a child? Yeah, most likely for a woman of ninety and a man of ninety -nine. What a ridiculous thing to predict! I am a worn out old woman, and I am to have this joy? Come on now, let's be real!

Then I heard the man say, *"Why did Sarah laugh and say, Will I really have a child now that I am old? Is anything too hard for the Lord? I will return to you at the appointed time next year, and Sarah will have a son."* (Ge 18:13, 14)

I was afraid, because I realized this man had heard me laugh, and I wondered if he might be a representative of the Lord. I came out from behind the flap of the tent and lied, "I did not laugh."

I must confess, however, that this incident left an impression on me, and a spark of hope was kindled. Amazing as it may seem, I did conceive and at the time indicated by the strange man who had visited us, I gave birth to a beautiful baby boy. Abraham gave him the name, Isaac, which means "he laughs."

I was elated and shouted out, "*God has brought me laughter, and everyone who hears about this will laugh with me. Who would have said to Abraham that Sarah would nurse children? Yet I have borne him a son in his old age.*" (Ge 21:6,7)

Isaac grew into a fine young boy. He was my pride and joy and the apple of his father's eye. He spent much time with his father learning how to care for the animals.

One day, when Isaac was about twelve years old, Abraham told me he was going on a trip and was going to take Isaac with him. I knew I would miss my boy but felt good about his taking this trip with his father. The next morning Abraham cut some wood, loaded up the donkey, took two servants, and he and Isaac set out on their trip. They were gone about a week and the morning after they got back, Abraham took off to attend to some business. Isaac and I were left in the tent alone. I asked Isaac where they had gone on the trip and what they done.

He began by telling me that they had gone to Mount Moriah, about sixty miles north of Beersheba where we were living at the time. Then, after hesitating, he said, "Dad told me that the Lord had spoken to him and instructed him to go to Mount Moriah and offer a sacrifice as a burnt offering."

He was trembling with emotion, but finally regained enough composure to continue, "When we drew near the place, he told the two servants, who had gone with us, to stay behind, because we were going on ahead to worship God. He asked me to carry the wood, and he carried the lighted torch and a knife.

"As we started up the side of the mountain, I asked him, 'Daddy, I have the wood, and you have the fire, but where is the lamb for the burnt offering?' He replied, 'God himself will provide the lamb for the sacrifice.' I thought this was strange, but you know how much faith Dad has, so I didn't question him anymore. We finally reached the top. He built an altar with the stones that were scattered around and arranged the wood…"

Isaac broke down weeping and rushed to my side. I hugged him tightly and asked him, "What happened next?"

"He tied me up, placed me on the altar, and…" Issac buried his head in my arms and sobbed. Then he said, "He raised the knife and was about to bring it down to my throat when we heard a loud voice from the clouds, 'Abraham! Abraham!' Dad answered, 'Here I am.' Then the voice said, 'Do not lay a hand on the boy. Do not do anything to him. Now I know that you fear God because you have not withheld from me your son, your only son.'

"Dad looked up, and there in the bushes nearby was a ram caught by its horns. He untied me, went over and took the ram, tied it up, laid it on the altar, lit the wood and we sacrificed it. When this was all over, I was trembling and Dad seemed so beside himself with joy and relief that we just stood there wrapped in each other's arms, crying and praising God."

I was horrified. I couldn't believe what I had heard and just held my son tightly. Finally, I let him go, and he ran outside. I sat there in the tent with terrible thoughts and emotions buzzing in my head. A dark cloud of anger appeared on the horizon of my spirit. I couldn't wait for Abraham to return for me to give him a piece of my mind.

When he arrived that afternoon, I rushed out to where he was tying up the donkey and blurted out, "Why didn't you tell me what you were going to do?"

"You would not have let me go if I had told you," he replied.

I continued: "I have often told you that the one thing I abhor, I detest, about the religion of our Canaanite neighbors is their human sacrifice, the sacrifice of their children to placate their horrible gods, and now you have stooped so low that you have adopted their practice. I can't believe it."

"God told me to do it," he said.

I grabbed his robe and, clenching my fist in front of his face, shouted, "What kind of a god have you taught us to worship anyway? A god just like the gods of the Canaanites, who is thirsty for human blood?"

"Sarah, Sarah!"

"Don't Sarah me. I'm angry! You not only humiliated me when you asked me to pose as your sister before Pharaoh and King Abimelech, and they took me into their harem, but now you have attempted to kill my only son. God was only playing with you in the worst way when he promised you a son only to do away with him."

Suddenly, I remembered how my husband had pleaded with God to spare Lot when the Lord was going to destroy Sodom, so I blurted out, "Why didn't you ask God to intervene in this matter like you did on behalf of Lot?

I kept on venting my anger and shouted, "How could you do this?"

My husband grabbed my arms and said, "Sarah, stop it! Stop it right now, and listen to me! I did this because I believed with all my heart that God would provide for the sacrifice, even to the point of believing that God could raise our son from the dead. Let me assure you that I, too, abhor the human sacrifices of the Canaanites as much as you do. But tell me, have you ever heard of one of their gods providing a lamb to impede a human sacrifice? Tell me!"

I thought about what he said and had to admit that none of the Canaanite gods had ever stopped the sacrifice of a child by providing a lamb.

The he added, "Our God, our merciful and gracious God, did not permit me to sacrifice Isaac. He provided a lamb."

A few moments later, I asked, "But I still don't understand why he instructed you to sacrifice our son?"

After a long pause, he replied, "I have been wondering if perhaps, through this experience, God wanted to show us how much he too abhors the Canaanite custom of sacrificing children."

I had not thought about that.

Then he added, "And perhaps also because he wanted to test me, to see if I loved him so much that I would give him that which I most dearly love. One night, on the trip coming home, we were sleeping out under the stars, when an angel of the Lord spoke to me again, and said, *I swear by myself, declares the Lord, that because you have done this and have not withheld your son, your only son, I will surely bless you and make your descendants as numerous as the stars in the sky and as the sand on the seashore. Your descendants will take possession of the cities of their enemies, and through your offspring all the nations of the earth will be blessed, because you have obeyed me."* (Ge 22:16-18)

I wondered, if God had asked me to give up my son, would I have obeyed?

2

ELIEZER'S MOST DIFFICULT TASK

Genesis 24

Many years ago, when Abraham and his caravan were traveling south from Haran, he stopped in the city of Damascus, and he and his family spent the night in our home. I, Eliezer, was a restless teenager. That evening, as we sat around the table, he told us about the strange God who had promised to bless him, to show him where he should go, and to make of his descendants a great nation, who would bless all the nations of the world. I decided to join his caravan as his servant.

I traveled with him to the land of Canaan, and when, because of famine, he had to go to Egypt, I also accompanied him. I was with him when he settled in Hebron and later had to rescue his nephew, Lot, who had been captured by a neighboring king. I was with him when his son Isaac was born and later accompanied the two when they went to Mount Moriah. I was with him when his wife Sarah died, and I helped him arrange for the purchase of the cave of Machpelah, near the oak of Mamre, which he used as his family tomb.

I became his most trusted servant. One time, before Isaac was born, he confided in me that if he had no heir, I would inherit his estate. I have administered his wealth, protected his gold and silver, coordinated the work of his many servants, and cared for his cattle, sheep, goats and camels.

My master is now very old and feeble. One afternoon, not long ago, he called for me to come to his tent. He asked me to draw near to his side and, in a faint and wavering voice, said, *Put your hand under my thigh.* (This is a custom we have when a man asks another man to solemnly promise him to do something for him.) *I want you to swear by the Lord, the God of heaven and the God of earth, that you will not get a wife for my son from the daughters of the Canaanites, among whom I am living, but will go to my country and my own relatives and get a wife for my son Isaac.* (Ge 24:3,4)

In our society, a father is supposed to select his son's wife, and it became clear to me that this was a great concern for him. He did not want Isaac to marry a Canaanite woman and be influenced by some of the detestable customs of her people. Abraham is too old to make the long trip to Haran, so he was entrusting me with the task.

I asked him, "What if the woman is unwilling to come back with me to this land? Shall I then take your son back to the country you came from?"

He paused to regain some strength and then said, "The Lord God who called me from my father's household and country, and who promised to give this land to my descendants, will send his angel before you to get a wife for my son. If she is unwilling to come with you, you will be released from this oath."

I agreed to go, put my hand under his thigh, and swore to him I would carry out his wish.

Because this was probably the most delicate mission my master had ever sent me on., I wanted to carry it out faithfully. So I made careful preparations. I selected ten of the finest camels and loaded them with provisions and gifts of gold and silver jewelry, the finest blankets, colorful shawls and draperies, and all kinds of tasty dried fruits. I asked a few of the younger servants to accompany me, and when we were ready to leave, I went to Abaham's tent, knelt down beside him and asked him to bless me.

During the long trip to the region of Aram Naharaim, I had plenty of time to consider how I would determine which was the right girl. I felt that I needed some clear indication from the Lord and did not want to be swayed only by her looks. Perhaps, I could conceive a plan whereby she would reveal something of her inner character. Once knowing who the girl was, I would have to woo her for my master's son -- no small task!

When I drew near to the community of Nahor and approached a spring, which serves as the town well, I had the camels kneel. It was evening, the time when the women came to draw water.

I knelt in prayer and said, "*O God, God of my master Abraham, make things go smoothly this day; treat my master well! As I stand here by the spring while the young women of the town come out to get water, let the girl to whom I say, 'lower your jug and give me a drink,' and who answers, 'Drink, and let me also water your camels' -- let her be the woman you have picked out for your servant Isaac. Then I'll know that your're working graciously behind the scenes for my master.*" (Ge 24:12-14 MSG)

I had no sooner finished my prayer, than I looked up and saw a stunningly beautiful girl come to the spring to fill her jug. As she was about to leave, I ran up to her and asked, "*Please, can I have a sip of water from your jug?*" (Ge 24:17 MSG)

She replied, "Of course," and she held the jug so that I could drink.

When I had satisfied my thirst, she said, "I'll be glad to get some water for your camels."

She promptly emptied her jug into the trough and ran back to the well to fill it time and again, until all the camels had been satisfied. I watched in silent admiration. Could she be God's answer to my prayer? Has he crowned my trip with success? If so, now comes the hard part -- how to woo her.

I searched in one of my bags, pulled out a gold nose ring weighing a fourth of an ounce and two bracelets weighing four ounces, and gave them to her. I inquired about her family, who her father was, and whether there was room in her father's house for us all to stay overnight.

She responded, "I am the daughter of Bethuel, the son of Nahor and Milkah. You're welcome to spend the night at our house. We have plenty of room, and there is straw and feed for the camels."

I was overjoyed, for I knew that Nahor was Abraham's brother. I bowed down in worship to the God of my master, who, I might add, has become my Lord also. I lifted up my spirit in prayer, "Blessed be the Lord, the God of Abraham. How good you have been to my master, and how good you have been to me, leading me right to his brother's house!"

The girl rushed back to town to share the news of my arrival, and while I was still standing near the well, amazed at what God had done and pondering what I should do next, her brother Laban came running out, embraced me, and said, "Welcome, you blessed of God, come with me, we are preparing a place for you, the men with you and the camels."

At the house, Laban introduced me to his father, Bethuel, his mother and the other members of the family. Their servants brought straw and fodder for the camels and water for me to wash my feet, while my companions began unloading the camels.

Laban and his wife prepared a sumptuous supper, but before we began to eat, I stood up and said: "I can't start eating until I have told you my story."

Laban urged me to continue, and I began:

"I'm the servant of Abraham. God has blessed him -- he's a great man; the Lord has given him sheep and cattle, camels and donkeys, silver and gold, and a houseful of servants, but he had no heirs. Then Sarah, my master's wife, gave him a son in her old age, and Abraham has left everything to his son. My master made me promise that I would not get a wife for his son from the women of Canaan where we live. He told me to go to his father's house and get a wife for Isaac from among his relatives. I asked him what I should do if the girl wouldn't come with me? He said he was sure that God, who has led him and blessed him so abundantly, would send his angel and arrange things in such a way that I would be able to bring back a wife for his son from among his extended family. He also said that if I were not successful in this venture, I would be free from the oath.

"Late this afternoon, I arrived at the spring and prayed to the Lord, asking him to work things out in the delicate task my master had given me. I told him that if a young woman comes to the well to draw water, and I ask her to give me drink, she not only gives me a drink but also waters the camels, let that woman be the wife God has chosen for my master's son.

"When I had finished praying, Rebekah came with a jug on her shoulder and after she had drawn water, I asked her to please give me a drink. She graciously held out her jug, gave me a drink, and immediately offered to water my camels. I asked her about her family, and she told me she is the daughter of Bethuel, the son of Nahor and Milcah. Then I gave her a gold nose ring and bracelets and praised the God of my master, Abraham, who has led me straight to the door of my master's family and to the future wife for his son.

"*Now, tell me what you are going to do. If you plan to respond with a generous yes, tell me. But if not, tell me plainly so I can figure out what to do next.*" (Ge 24:49 MSG)

Laban and his father, Bethuel, told me they think this is from God, and so they can't say yes or no, but add that Rebekah is mine, and I can take her to be Isaac's wife.

I was grateful and bowed my head in worship before the Lord. I unwrapped the gifts I had brought and gave them to Rebekah, to her brother and her mother. Then, my companions and I sat around with Rebekah's family and enjoyed the feast they had prepared.

The next morning, the sun had barely risen when I was up and ready to go. I asked them to bless me and send me on my way back to Abraham, but Laban and his mother hesitated and finally said, "Let Rebekah stay for a couple of weeks before you take her with you."

I objected and said emphatically, "I can't wait. God has had a hand in this, and I must be on my way back to my master."

They decided to call Rebekah and see what she wanted to do. When she came and they asked her, she responded firmly, "I am ready and want to go now."

Rebekah gathered her things, and she and her family, along with me and my men, formed a circle. Laban blessed her with these words:

You're our sister-- live bountifully!
And your children, triumphantly!
(Ge 24:60 MSG)

Then Rebekah, her nurse and her servants, mounted our camels and we were off.

Many days later, as we were approaching the Negev, the area where Isaac lives, we saw a man out in the field, who, when he saw us, came running. When Rebekah saw him coming towards her, she got down from her camel and asked me who the man was.

I said to her, "That's my master's son Isaac."

She covered her face with her veil. I got off my camel and ran towards Isaac and embraced him. As we walked to the village, I told him the whole story of my adventure.

He took Rebekah into his tent, and they became husband and wife. "Mission accomplished," I said to myself.

3

JACOB MEETS HIS MATCH

Genesis 25:19-34; 27; 29:1-30;
30:25-43; 31-33

My name is Jacob. I am the son of Isaac and Rebekah. I have a twin brother named Esau. I want to tell you about an amazing experience I had that transformed my life. For you to understand how this experience impacted me, I need to share with you the story of my life.

My mother told me that when the time came for her to give birth, my brother, Esau, came out of her womb first, and I came out second holding onto his heel. She often reminded me that before I was born, the Lord had promised her that there were two peoples in her womb, and that one would be stronger than the other, the older one would serve the younger one.

My brother was red and ruddy. As he grew up, he enjoyed the outdoors, became a skillful hunter, and was my father's favorite. I, on the other hand, favored a more sedentary life style, liked to stick around the tents, enjoyed cooking, and became my mother's favorite. She never missed an opportunity to remind me that even though my brother was the strong athletic type, I needed to assert myself because I was really the stronger one.

This stuck with me. One time when I was cooking up some stew, Esau came in from the fields famished and asked me for some. I saw my opportunity and asked him to trade his rights as the first-born for some of my stew. He couldn't see what value there was in a birthright, when what he needed most was food, so he agreed. I saw he was dead serious about this. I made him swear with an oath, and he exchanged his birthright for my stew of lentils. When I told my mother about this, she celebrated it, and I learned that I could get what I wanted by scheming. This lesson was only reinforced by what happened years later.

I was forty at the time, and my father was old and blind. One day, my mother overheard him tell Esau:, *"I am now an old man and don't know the day of my death. Now then get your equipment --your quiver and bow-- and go out into the open country to hunt some wild game for me. Prepare me the kind of tasty food I like and bring it to me to eat, so that I may give you my blessing before I die."* (Ge 27:2-4)

After my brother left, my mother took me aside and told me what she had heard and then said, *"Now, my son, listen carefully and do what I tell you. Go out to the flock and bring me two choice young goats, so I can prepare some tasty food for your father just the way he likes it. Then take it to your father to eat, so that he may give you his blessing before he dies."* (Ge 27:8-10)

I objected. I told her that Esau was hairy, and that Dad would see I was tricking him. Instead of blessing me, he would curse me. She was not dissuaded and let me know that she would let the curse fall on herself. I did what she told me to do, and when she had prepared the food, she got some of Esau's clothes, put them on me, and covered my hands and neck with goatskins.

I went in to my father's tent and said, "I am Esau your first-born son. I did what you told me to do. Sit up and eat some of this delicious meat that I have prepared for you, and give me your blessing."

Dad asked me how I had found game so quickly, and I told him that the Lord had given me success in the hunt. Since he remembered I had tricked Esau out of his birthright, he said, "Come close so that I can touch you and know whether you are truly Esau."

I drew close to him, and after he touched me, he said, "The voice is Jacob's, but the hands are Esau's."

I then gave him the grilled meat, some bread, and a little wine. After he had eaten, he asked me to come near to him, so he could kiss me. When he caught the smell of Esau's clothes, he put his hands on my head and blessed me with these words,

"Ah, the smell of my son
is like the smell of a field
that the Lord has blessed.
May God give you heaven's dew
and earth's richness--
an abundance of grain and new wine."
(Ge 27:27-28)

I had barely left Dad's tent when Esau returned from hunting. He prepared his animal, cooked a hearty meal, and took it to Dad. I knew what was going to happen, and it wasn't going to be pleasant. As I stood behind the tent, I heard my father's trembling voice tell Esau he had already eaten and then say, *"Your brother came deceitfully and took your blessing."* (Ge 27:35)

Esau let out a wild cry of anger and began to sob violently. I heard him plead with Dad to give him a blessing, too, and finally Dad said,

"Your dwelling will be
away from the earth's richness,
away from the dew of heaven above.
You will live by the sword
and you will serve your brother."
(Ge 27:39, 40a)

Esau let it be known that after our father's death, which he thought would not be too far in the future, he would kill me. When Mother learned of Esau's intention, she urged me to leave as soon as possible, to go far away to the north, to Haran, the village of her brother Laban.

I made the long journey and arrived at a well in an open field near a village. A number of shepherds were sitting around waiting for the flocks of sheep to be gathered, so they could water them. I asked them where they were from, and they said, "We're from Haran."

I then asked them if they knew a man by the name of Laban, and they answered that they did. When I inquired about his health, they said he was well.

Just then, they looked up, and one of them said, "Look, here comes his daughter Rachel with their flock."

When Rachel came up to the well, I removed the stone that covered the well and watered her sheep. I went over to her, with tears of joy running down my cheeks, threw my arms around her, kissed her, and told her that I was her cousin. On hearing this, she rushed back to the village, and soon her father, my Uncle Laban, came running. He embraced me and took me to his house where that evening I told them my story.

Let me tell you that I met my match in Uncle Laban. He had two daughters, the older one, Leah, had pleasing eyes, but Rachel had a lovely figure and was stunning in appearance. Soon, I fell madly in love with Rachel. I had been working around the place helping out in whatever way I could, when one day Uncle Laban asked me what he could do to pay me for my work. I told him I was so in love with his daughter, Rachel, that I was willing to work seven years for him if he would give her to me in marriage. He agreed.

The seven years seemed like seven days because of my love for Rachel. When it was time to consummate the marriage, Uncle Laban held a big feast and invited all the people from the village. I really don't know what happened. Maybe I had a little too much wine, because when I awoke the next morning, it was Leah who was in bed with me.

As soon as I had breakfast, I went looking for my uncle, and when I found him, I said, "Hey, what's this you've done to me. I worked faithfully for seven years for Rachel, and you give me Leah. Why have you tricked me?"

He answered, "It is not our custom to give the younger daughter in marriage before the older one. Finish this week of honeymoon, and then I'll give you Rachel, but you must give me another seven years of labor."

I was furious, but my love for Rachel was so great that I agreed. Through those seven years I learned the value of persistence. If you persevere in what you want, eventually you will get it.

I became the patriarch of a large family, twelve sons in all, and began to yearn to return to my people in Canaan. When I expressed my desire to my uncle, he asked me to work for him a little longer because he had been blessed and prospered while I tended his flocks. Although he said I could have the spotted animals, he sent them to graze elsewhere.

I had to devise a scheme whereby my sheep and goats gave birth to spotted young. As my flocks increased, my self-confidence grew. At the end of six years, I had plenty of spotted sheep and goats, donkeys and even camels.

Uncle Laban's sons began to spread rumors that I was prospering at the expense of their father. I remembered that I had a dream years before at Bethel where I saw a stair-case reaching up to heaven with angels ascending and descending. The Lord God was standing at the top telling me that he promised to give me the land on which I was lying and that my descendants would spread out to the four corners of the earth and be a blessing to all people. Remembering this dream, I decided it was time for me to leave. I called Rachel and Leah and told them that God had instructed me to go back to Canaan. We made preparations, and in a few days, the caravan of my family, servants and animals were on our way.

When my uncle realized we were gone, he pursued us until he caught up to us where we had camped in the region of Gilead and poured out a sob story that ran like this:

"What have you done? You've deceived me, and you carried off my daughters like captives in war... Why didn't you tell me, so I could send you away with joy and singing to the music of timbrels and harps? You didn't even let me kiss my grandchildren and my daughters goodbye. You have done a foolish thing..." After a pause he added, *"Why did you steal my gods?"* (Ge 31:24-28, 30)

I didn't know until later that Rachel really had stolen the family idols, so I told my uncle to search to see if he could find anything that we had stolen. Rachel had hidden the idols under the camel's saddle she was sitting on, and her father did not find them.

After he came back I said, "If you found anything put it here in front of us all…"

When he didn't produce anything, I blew up. "For twenty years I have served you, fourteen for Rachel and Leah, and six caring for your flocks. I spent weeks away from my family, endured the heat of the sun and the chill of the night. If it had not been for the God of my fathers, you would have sent me away empty-handed."

After a lengthy discussion, we reached the agreement that neither of us would trespass on the other's land, and we would respect each other. We put a heap of stones around a large stone as a witness to our agreement. My uncle embraced and kissed his daughters and all his grand-children and started on his journey back to Haran.

I and my people continued on our journey south. When we were close to Canaan, I sent some of the servants ahead to inform Esau that we were returning, and I hoped to gain his favor. When the men returned, they informed me that my brother was coming to meet us with four hundred men.

I confess I was scared. I decided to divide the whole caravan into two groups, thinking that if Esau destroyed one group, the other might be able to escape. I also separated two hundred female goats and twenty male goats, the same number of ewes and rams, and a selection of camels, donkeys, cows and bulls. I put servants in charge of the various herds and instructed each servant to say, as they approached Esau, "These are a gift from your servant Jacob who is coming behind us," and sent them off.

During the twenty years of my exile my communion with the Lord had been sporadic, but that night I prayed as I had never prayed before, "O God of my father Abraham, God of my father Isaac, Lord, you who said to me, 'Go back to your country and your relatives, and I will make you prosper,' I am unworthy of all the kindness and faithfulness you have shown your servant. I had only my staff when I crossed this Jordan, but now I have become two camps. Save me, I pray, from the hand of my brother Esau, for I am afraid he will come and attack me, and also the mothers and children. (Ge 32:9-11)

Later, on that moonlit night, I was standing by the wadi Jabbok (wadi is the word we use for gulley), listening to the water as it cascaded over the rocks and watching the torrent as it churned its winding way down to the Jordan River. I thought, "So will I, opposed though I be, win my way, by the circuitous routes of craft or by the impetuous rush of courage, into the land whither that stream is going." (from Marcus Dods)

Suddenly, I felt someone grab me from behind, knock me down and pin me to the ground. The strength I had acquired through many years out in the fields served me well, and I was able to wrestle with the man all night. At dawn, before the sun came up, when he saw he could not overpower me, he threw my hip out of joint, damaged the muscle, and rendered me powerless. He said, "Let me go."

And I replied, *"I will not let you go until you bless me."*

He asked me what my name was and I told him, Jacob.

Then he said, *"Your name will no longer be Jacob, but Israel, because you have struggled with God and with humans and have overcome."* (Ge 32:26-28)

I asked him what his name was, but he wouldn't tell me. He then blessed me and left.

Just as the sun rose, I stood up, crossed the stream, and slowly began walking along the path towards the inevitable encounter with my brother. The pain in my hip was so intense I had to sit down under a tree. Thoughts were cascading around in my head as I tried to make sense out of this strange experience. I finally came to the conclusion that I had come face to face with God, and yet he had spared my life.

He said I had struggled with God and humans and had overcome, but the truth is God struggled with me and overcame me. I was forced to rethink my whole life and realized that just as I wrestled with God, so I have wrestled life with craftiness, courage and especially self-confidence. My whole life has been the wrestling match of a self-confident individual who was persuaded he could get whatever he set out to achieve by clever, devious and consistent self-effort. Ultimately, I wrestled with God, who set out to break my self-sufficiency in order to bestow upon me authentic divine wisdom, humility and strength. When I saw how foolish and vain my stubborn persistence had been and that I could do nothing, I ceased wrestling and prayed, "I will not let you go until you bless me." I met my match in this struggle with God.

But in the encounter, God broke my pride with a blow that left its permanent mark on me, a mark which I now consider the sign of his blessing. This mark never fails to remind me of how he transformed me. I have often wondered if everyone who has an encounter with the living God is marked for life.

I named the place of my struggle Peniel, which means "the face of God." I got up and continued limping humbly along the path to meet the brother I had wronged.

4

EVIL TURNED INTO GOOD

Genesis 37, 42-45

I am the oldest of my father Jacob's twelve sons, and my name is Reuben (Ge 35:23-26). I was born in Haran, the town in northwestern Mesopotamia where my mother Leah is from. This was some years before my parents and their offspring moved to Canaan. I think you will find the story of my family interesting because of something rather extraordinary that happened to us.

Dad had a special affection for my younger half-brother Joseph. It was very apparent to all of us that he was my father's favorite. One time, Dad made a beautiful robe for Joseph and gave it to him on one of his birthdays. Joseph became sort of stuck on himself and knew he could get away with most anything. Since I am the oldest and my place in the family was secure, this didn't bother me, but my brothers grew very jealous of him. Various times, when we returned from tending the sheep, he would tell Dad that we had let the sheep wander off and were not caring for them properly. This only made things worse, and my brothers developed a strong animosity towards him.

One morning, at breakfast, Joseph told us he had dreamed that we were all binding sheaves of grain, and his sheaf stood upright while all our sheaves bowed down to his. Then, on another occasion, he said he dreamed that the sun and moon and eleven stars were all bowing down to him.

Dad severely reprimanded him and said, "What is this that you are telling us, that your brothers and I will actually bow down before you?"

You can imagine how we received these dreams. They even upset me. My brothers were very angry and from that time on could not say a kind word about him.

We had to take the sheep to graze near Shechem, which is between thirty and forty miles north of Hebron where we were living at the time. One afternoon, about a month after we had been gone, we saw Joseph, in the distance, coming towards us. He was wearing his beautiful robe of many colors.

I heard one of my brothers whisper, *"Here comes that dreamer! Come now, let's kill him and throw him into one of those cisterns and say that a ferocious animal devoured him. Then we'll see what comes of his dreams."* (Ge 37:19, 20)

They all agreed, but I objected and said, "Let's not kill him, but rather let's throw him into one of the pits here and not harm him."

When Joseph arrived, they stripped him of his robe, bound him, and threw him into one of the cisterns. While we were having our meal, I had to go check on the flocks. When I returned, I went to see if I could rescue Joseph and found the cistern empty. I was distressed and ran back to my brothers to ask what they had done to Joseph.

Judah informed me that while I was gone, a caravan of Ishmaelites had passed by on their way south to Egypt to sell their spices, and he had suggested they sell Joseph to the traders. They made me swear to secrecy and threatened to harm me if I told anyone what they had done. Then, they slaughtered a goat and splattered the blood on Joseph's robe.

When we returned to Hebron, our father asked where Joseph was. We gathered around him. Judah took out Joseph's robe, showed it to our father and said, *"We found this. Examine it and see whether it is your son's robe."* (Ge 37:32)

When Dad held it up, he could see that it was splattered with blood. He shook violently, and he cried out, *"This is my son's robe! Some ferocious animal has devoured him. Joseph has surely been torn to pieces."* (Ge 37:33)

Judah embraced Dad and said, "That is exactly what happened. We found the robe on the side of the road."

My father tore his clothes, put on sackcloth, covered his head with ashes and went into a deep depression. We all tried to comfort him, but he would only say, "No, *I will continue to mourn until I join my son in the grave.*"

He didn't recover from this tragedy for many years.

Sometime later there was a severe famine in Canaan. The winter rains didn't come, the crops failed, the grass in the fields dried up, and the animals began to die. We heard rumors that there was grain in Egypt, and Dad urged us to go and see if we could buy some. We loaded the donkeys with what provisions we could come up with and some bags of silver and set off. We left our youngest brother, Benjamin, to take care of Dad.

In Egypt, we discovered that the famine was widespread and there were mobs of people from all over the region searching for food. We waited our turn and were received by the man who seemed to be the chief administrative officer in charge of selling the grain. He asked us where we were from and then accused us of being spies who had come to scout out the land and see where its defenses were weak.

Judah, our spokesman, replied, "No, my lord, your servants have come to buy food. We are honest men, not spies. We were twelve sons of one man who lives in Canaan. Our youngest brother stayed with our father, and one disappeared many years ago."

The administrator insisted, "It is just as I told you: You are spies! And this is how I will test you. As surely as Pharaoh lives, you will not leave this place unless your youngest brother comes here. One of you must go back to get your brother while the rest of you are held here in prison."

After being imprisoned for three days, the man called us into his presence and said, "I've changed my mind. I will keep one of you in prison, and the rest of you will take grain and go back to your starving families. But you must bring your youngest brother to me so that your story may be verified, and you won't die."

As we were discussing among ourselves whether we should do this, Simeon said, "God is punishing us for the way we treated Joseph. That is why this trouble has come upon us."

And I added, "Didn't I tell you not to harm to the boy? You wouldn't listen to me! God has called us to account."

The man saw us discussing. He turned away and wiped his face. Then he took Simeon, had him bound and put back in prison. He gave orders to fill our sacks with grain which we loaded onto the donkeys and left.

That night, when we camped at an oasis, I opened my sack to get some grain for my donkey, and there on top of the grain was my bag of silver. I turned to my brothers and said, "Look what I found in my sack."

We were shocked and wondered whether we should return to Egypt but finally decided to go on.

When we got back home and emptied our sacks of grain, out came the pouch of silver from each sack. Were we ever upset! We didn't know what to think.

Judah reported to Dad, "The Egyptian administrator would not believe our story. He accused us being spies, and held Simeon in prison. He insisted that we had to bring our youngest brother to him as proof that we were telling the truth, and only then he would release Simeon."

The drought continued, and, when we had consumed all the grain we had brought, Dad wanted us to return to Egypt to get more grain.

We reminded him that the administrator had warned us that we would not see his face again unless our brother was with us. Then Judah added, "If you will send Benjamin with us, we'll go, but if you won't, we refuse to go."

Dad was vehement, "I will not let Benjamin go with you. His brother Joseph is dead. If harm comes to Benjamin on the journey, my gray head will go down to the grave."

After a pause, he said, "Why did you bring this trouble on me? Why did you tell the man you had a brother?"

Judah explained to Dad, "The man asked us if we had another brother, and if our father was still living. We were simply answering his questions and had no idea he would insist we bring Benjamin with us."

Finally, seeing Dad's resistance, Judah added, "Send Benjamin along with us, so we may leave at once and get food for our families. I, myself, will guarantee to bring him back, and if you don't see him here before you safe and sound, you can hold me personally responsible. I will bear the blame all my life."

Dad wavered but finally answered, "OK, what must be, must be. Get the best we have, a little honey, spices, pistachio nuts, and almonds as gifts for the administrator. Take double the amount of silver to pay back the silver that was in your sacks. Maybe they made a mistake. Take Benjamin and go at once, and may Almighty God grant you mercy before the administrator so he may let you bring back Simeon and Benjamin."

We hurried down to Egypt. When we met the administrator, and he saw that we had Benjamin with us, he instructed his steward to take us to his house. The servants were to slaughter an animal and prepare a meal for us.

We were scared stiff because we thought that he wanted to punish us for the silver that we had found in our sacks after the first trip. So, just as we arrived at the door of the house, Judah explained to the steward, "When we came the first time to buy food, we paid for it with silver, and on the way back, we discovered the same amount of silver in each of our sacks. We have brought back that silver and have more with which to buy more grain."

The steward told us not to be afraid, for God had given us back our silver as a bonus and the account was settled. Then, he brought out Simeon. Were we ever glad to see him! We rushed over, and each of us gave him a big hug.

The steward called a servant to take care of our donkeys while he ushered us into the house. He gave us basins of water to cool off our feet and made us comfortable. When the administrator arrived, we bowed respectfully and presented our gifts to him. He asked us about our father, and then, as he looked at Benjamin, he said, "Is this the youngest brother you told me about?"

Placing his hand on Benjamin's shoulder, he added, "God bless you my son."

He suddenly rushed out of the room with no explanation, but after
a few minutes, he returned wiping his face with a towel, and ordered the
steward to serve the food. He sat by himself. We were seated around
a table facing him, and the other people, who were present, at another
table. We were served platters full of delicious meat, but I noticed that
the steward served Benjamin extra large helpings. During our feast, I saw
that the administrator drank his wine out of a large beautifully decorated
silver chalice.

We slept comfortably that night. We arose before sunrise, loaded our
donkeys with the sacks of grain, and started for home. We had barely
reached the edge of the city when the steward came running up to us,
and said, "Why have you repaid evil for good. My master's silver chalice
is missing. You must have stolen it."

"How could we do such a thing?" I asked. Then added, "We brought
you back the money we found in our sacks and have paid for this grain
with more silver. Why would we want to steal from your master? Be
assured that if the chalice is found in possession of one of us, that one
should die, and the rest of us will be your slaves."

"All right," he said.

We unloaded the donkeys, and he began inspecting each sack,
beginning with mine, since I am the oldest. The last sack to be opened
was Benjamin's, and when the steward poured out the grain, out came the
chalice. We cried out in despair and tore our clothes. There was nothing
to do but load our donkeys and go back to the administrator's house.

He was there, waiting for us, and said, "What have you done? Don't
you know that a man in my position can tell when something like this
is done?"

We all prostrated ourselves before him, and Judah replied, "What
can we say? We can't prove our innocence. God has uncovered our guilt.
We are all our master's slaves."

"Oh no," he said. "Only the one in whose sack the chalice was found
will become my slave. The rest of you can go home."

I shuddered at the prospect of telling Dad that Benjamin was a slave
in Egypt.

My brother, Judah, stood up, slowly walked towards the administrator, bowed and said, "My Lord, I am not worthy to address you since you are equal to Pharaoh, so please pardon your servant's boldness. You asked us if we had a father and a younger brother, and we answered that we did, and that our father was aged and loved his youngest son. You then told us that to prove we were honest men, we had to bring our youngest brother, and that if we did not bring him, you would not attend to us. When we reported this to our father, he said, 'Remember that Rachel, my wife, bore me two sons -- one was torn to pieces by an animal, and if you take his brother from me, I will surely go to my grave.' So if the boy is not with us when we return to our father, he will die.

"Let me remain as your slave in place of the boy, and let him return with his brothers. How can I go back to my father without the boy? No! Do not let me see the grief which will take my father to his grave."

Since Judah was the one who had suggested that Joseph be sold to the Ishmaelite traders, I was pleased that it was he who offered to take the place of Benjamin.

Suddenly, the administrator seemed to lose control of himself. He ordered all the servants out of the room and began to weep. He rushed towards Judah, and wrapped him in his arms. In the midst of his sobbing, he cried out, "I am Joseph!"

These words left me dazed. I could not believe what I was hearing. He went around embracing each one of us, and then said, "I am your brother Joseph, the one you sold into Egypt! Don't be disturbed and angry with yourselves for selling me here, for it was God who sent me here ahead of you to save your lives."

After he had kissed and hugged Benjamin, he said, "The famine will continue for five more years. It was God who sent me here to provide food for all of you and your animals. You can see for yourselves that it is me, Joseph, who is really speaking to you. Now, hurry back home, get my father and bring him to me.

I couldn't contain myself, so I ran up to Joseph, held him in my arms in a firm embrace, and exclaimed, "May the Lord our God be praised, for he has turned our evil into good. In spite of our wicked intentions, he preserved your life so that through you he could preserve our lives."

5

THE STORY OF AN APPRENTICE

Exodus 17:8-16; 19, 32, 33:7-23; Numbers 13, 21:1-13; 27:12-32

One sunny fall afternoon, Moses gathered all the people of Israel in solemn assembly at the base of Mt. Pisgah. He addressed them with these words:

"I am now one hundred twenty years old, and I am not able to lead you any longer. I am not to cross the Jordan to take possession of the land the Lord our God promised to our ancestors, but he will cross over ahead of you and will deliver the inhabitants of the land into your hand. Do not be afraid. The Lord your God goes with you; he will never leave you nor forsake you."

Then Moses summoned me, Joshua, to stand before him, Eleazar the priest, and all the people, and said, "You have been appointed by God to lead this people and take possession of the land God has promised them. Be strong and courageous. Don't be afraid. Don't worry, for the Lord has promised to never leave you or abandon you."

He laid his hands on me, gave me his blessing, and commissioned me. I trembled at the awesome task God had placed in my hands and wanted to be faithful and responsible in carrying out that which was expected of me.

I knew this heavy responsibility was coming, for I had been Moses' aide for many years. During that time God, was carefully preparing me to take Moses' place. I want to share with you some of the memorable experiences and lessons I learned during those years of apprenticeship.

I first came to Moses' attention shortly after we left Egypt when a band of Amalekites attacked us as we were crossing the Desert of Shur. When he asked me to choose some men and repel the attack, I was convinced God would give us success in battle, for I had seen how God had provided water, manna and quail for us,

Three months after leaving Egypt, we arrived at the base of Mt. Sinai, where we set up a permanent camp. We had been there three days, when a thick cloud covered the mountain. There was thunder and lightning, the mountain shook, and smoke billowed as if it were a volcano erupting. With fear and trembling, Moses and I started up the mountain, but only he entered the thick cloud. God must have had a lot to tell him, for he was there many days. I grew weary and had to scavenge for food. Finally, I saw him coming down, carrying two huge stone tablets inscribed on both sides. Moses told me that the finger of God had engraved the writing on the tablets and that these contained the basic principles of the law of God.

As we were descending the mountain, I heard the people shouting. Alarmed, I said, "It sounds to me like there is war in the camp."

Moses replied, "No, I don't hear the sound of arms. it sounds to me like wild exotic singing."

When we were about half way down, we saw all the people dancing in a frenzied manner around a golden calf which was up on a pedestal. Moses was so angry he threw the two tablets down the mountainside, and they broke in pieces. When we got to the camp, he took the calf, burned it in the fire, ground it to powder, mixed it in water, and made the people drink it.

Then he said to Aaron, his brother, "What did these people do that made you lead them into such terrible sin?"

Aaron answered, "You were gone so long, the people grew restless and wanted a god to lead them. So they gave me their gold jewelry. I threw it into the fire and out came the calf."

I almost laughed out loud when I heard this ridiculous response. I had seen the people shouting, running around wildly, totally out of control, and recognized the degrading effects of idolatry. From that day on, I have always abhorred idolatry. I determined then and there that as for me and my family we would always serve the Lord. Many years later, when we had taken possession of the land and the covenant was being renewed, but idolatry was still a problem, I challenged the people to choose between serving their idols or serving the living God. I affirmed once more, "as for me and my family we will serve the Lord."

Moses had a tent that he pitched outside the camp, called the "tent of meeting." I would go with him and stand outside while he would go in and meet with the Lord. A cloud would come down and cover the entrance. I could hear the conversation between Moses and the Lord, and it seemed to me that they spoke to each other face to face as friends. On one occasion I heard Moses say to the Lord, *If your Presence does not go with us, do not send us up from here.*

I heard the Lord's answer, "*I will do the very thing you have asked, because I am pleased with you and I know you by name.*" (Ex 33: 15, 17)

I realized that it was his intimate communion with the Lord that empowered Moses to lead the people with patience and fortitude. Many times, after he left the tent, I stayed behind and said to the Lord, "*If you are pleased with me, teach me your ways so I may know you and continue to find favor with you.* Teach me how to lead your people." (Ex 33:13) I also held on to his promise to go with us.

In preparation for the campaign to conquer the land of Canaan, I was one of the twelve men Moses chose to go and explore it. We were instructed to see if there were numerous inhabitants, or if the land was sparsely settled, whether the towns were fortified or un-walled, whether the soil was fertile, and whether there were any forests.

We explored the Negev as far as Hebron and went on up to the city of Hazor just beyond the Sea of Galilee. At the end of forty days, we returned carrying pomegranates, figs, and an enormous cluster of grapes hanging from a pole.

Moses gathered the whole Israelite community to hear our report. Ten of the men gave the majority report and informed the assembly that the land flowed with milk and honey (their expression for a prosperous land) and showed the fruit we had brought. But they recommended we not go up into the land because the people were very strong, the cities large and fortified. They emphasized that we seemed to be like grasshoppers in the presence of their men who were like giants. This was clearly an exaggeration.

My companion Caleb and I were extremely upset at this. We gave our minority report, informing the people that the land was exceedingly good, and we recommended that we immediately take possession of it. Caleb argued that we should not fear, for the Lord would lead us and give us success.

The majority report won. This displeased the Lord, and when he met Moses in the tent of meeting, he threatened to destroy the people.

I heard Moses argue with the Lord, "If you destroy your people, the Egyptians and the Canaanites will say that you were not able to bring your people into the land you had promised them," and, after a pause, he added, "You are slow to anger, you abound in love, so forgive the sin of these people, just as you have been forgiving them since they left Egypt."

The Lord replied that he would forgive the people, but would not allow any of those over twenty years of age, except Caleb and me, to enter the promised land. They would be destined to wander in the wilderness until they had all died.

What a severe lesson! We have been wandering around for many years because of the people's contempt of God and their refusal to believe he was able to lead them into the promised land just as he had delivered them from slavery in a different land. It is a fearful thing to disobey God and fall into his hands. I also learned how difficult it is to stand for what you believe when all those around you think you are wrong.

One of the strangest things happened while we were camped in the Desert of Sin near Kadesh-barnea. The people were again complaining and bickering about the lack of water. When the people began scheming against Moses and Aaron, I saw Moses and Aaron go into the tent of meeting and fall facedown before the Lord in frustration and supplication.

Then I heard the voice of the Lord, "Take your staff, gather the assembly together. Speak to the rock before their eyes, and it will pour out its water."

As they left the tent of meeting, I could tell Moses was very angry. He called the people together in front of the rock, and said, "OK, you rebels. We will bring water out of this rock for you."

Then he raised his arm and slammed the rock violently with his staff, not once but twice. Water gushed out, and the people drank and watered their animals.

The next time Moses came out from the tent of meeting after communing with the Lord, I could tell by the look on his face something was wrong. He told me sadly, "Today the Lord said to me, 'Because you did not trust me and did not respect my holiness in the presence of the people, and you vented your anger towards them, you will not lead the people into the land that I am giving them.'"

This troubled me greatly! I didn't think this was fair. Moses had intimate communion with the Lord as friend to friend, patiently leading the people who were constantly murmuring and bickering, carefully instructing them in the way of the Lord, and because of one violent outburst of anger was denied entrance to the promised land, denied reaching the goal he had been struggling towards all his life… this did not seem fair to me.

For several days, I could not get this incident out of my mind. This was not the first time I had seen Moses angry. He had been so mad when we came down from Mt. Sinai and saw the golden calf, that he broke the tablets of the law. The Lord did not punish him then. Why punish him now because of what happened at the rock? I realize that flying off the handle in public has dire consequences, but still, I could not make sense out of this.

There must be a difference in the anger Moses vented at the base of Mr. Sinai and the anger expressed at the Waters of Meribah. In the second instance, God said, "you didn't trust in me enough to honor me as holy." It is true that the Lord told him to <u>speak to the rock</u> and instead he <u>struck the rock.</u> Perhaps, in his anger he did not trust the Lord to bring forth water by merely speaking to it and felt he had to strike it.

I also wondered if in the first incident Moses' anger was holy anger directed against the idolatry of the people, but in the second, his anger was an expression of his frustration with God's people, maybe even frustration with God for continually testing his trust. Could it also be that in his frustration, he was actually angry with the Lord?

After mulling this over for a time, I gave voice to my secret prayer, "Oh Lord, preserve me from dishonoring you through anger and lack of trust."

Now, here I am, standing on the eastern bank of the Jordan River ready to cross over into Canaan. Again, I open my heart to the Lord and try to listen to his voice. I seem to hear him say to me, "Moses my servant is dead. You and all the people must get ready to cross the river to take possession of the land that I have promised them...As I was with Moses, so I will be with you; I will never leave you nor forsake you. Be strong and courageous."

6

HOW ISRAEL GOT A KING

1 Samuel 3, 8-10, 13-15

Let me have a few minutes of your time while I tell you the interesting story of the crisis that led to the Israelites demanding a king. It is also part of my personal story, so let me introduce myself and give you a brief summary of my life. My name is Samuel, and my parents were Elkanah and Hannah. We lived in the town of Ramah, in the hill country of Ephraim. My mother was childless, and one year, when she and my father went to Shiloh to worship the Lord, she prayed earnestly and made a vow to the Lord that if he would give her a son, she would dedicate him to the Lord. The Lord answered her prayer, and a year later I was born.

She fulfilled her vow, and, after she had spent the prescribed time nursing me, she took me to the house of the Lord in Shiloh. There she offered a young bull, a forty- pound bag of flour, and a skin of wine in gratitude. Then she presented me to Eli, the priest, for a lifetime of service to the Lord.

When I was about twelve years old, I had my first encounter with the Lord. I was sleeping in the house of the Lord near the Chest of God's Covenant when I heard a voice calling me. I got up and ran over to Eli and said, "Here, I am." He told me he had not called me and sent me back to bed. This happened again. The third time it happened, Eli told me to go lie down, and, if I heard the voice again, to say, "Speak, Lord, for your servant is listening." When I heard the voice, I answered as Eli had told me, and the Lord spoke to me. He told me that Eli's sons had done contemptible things, and, since Eli had not restrained them, he and his sons would be judged. The next morning, I feared to give this message to Eli, but after he urged me to tell him what the Lord had said, I told him everything.

In those days messages from the Lord were scarce, but as the Lord continued to speak to me, I matured in my commitment to him. After Eli died, all Israel came to recognize me as the priest and prophet.

The principal problem I had to deal with during my long ministry as prophet of the Lord was the idolatry of the people. Though they professed to be the Lord's chosen people, they hid idols of foreign gods in their homes. At times they publicly worshipped the female deities of the Canaanite people. Every year, on my circuit around the towns and villages of Israel, I saw evidence of idolatry: rocks set up as altars, poles to female deities, and other such things. I preached on the verses in the law handed down by Moses, "You shall have no other gods besides me," and, "You shall not make for yourself an image in the form of anything in heaven above or on the earth beneath or in the waters below. You shall not bow down to them or worship them." (Dt 5:7,8) I was dismayed that my words seldom struck a responsive chord.

When I no longer had the energy to walk all over Canaan from Bethel to Gilgal in my annual visits, I decided to appoint my sons as priests in my place. This was a serious mistake, for my sons took advantage of their position and accepted bribes and corrupted justice. I am afraid this was the result of my not spending quality time with my family and mentoring my sons. This led to the crisis I mentioned.

When the elders of people saw my sons' crooked ways, they gathered and came to me at Ramah and said, "Look, you're an old man now, and your sons are a mess. We'll tell you what you should do. You should appoint a king to rule over us, just like the other nations have."

I was devastated: Appoint a king!? No way!

I was deeply hurt and upset, for as their priest and prophet, I had offered their sacrifices to the Lord and proclaimed his message to them.

I had spent my life traveling all over the land mediating their disputes, dispensing justice, and had even led them in battle against the Philistines. Now they wanted a king. No king would ever do for the people what I had done for them.

That night I walked out in the fields and spent a long time looking up at the stars. As I prayed, a cloud covered Orion's belt, and I heard the Lord say to me: *"Go ahead and do what they're asking. They are not rejecting you. They've rejected me as their King. From the day I brought them out of Egypt until this very day they've behaved like this, leaving me for other gods. And now they're doing it to you. So let them have their own way. But warn them of what they're in for. Tell them the way kings operate..."* (1Sa 8:7-9 MSG)

I called for a solemn assembly, and when the people had gathered, I said to them: *"This is the way the kind of king you're talking about operates. He'll take your sons and make soldiers of them... He'll put others to forced labor on his farms, plowing and harvesting, and others to making either weapons of war or chariots in which he can ride in luxury. He'll put your daughters to work as beauticians and waitresses and cooks. He'll conscript your best fields, vineyards, and orchards and hand them over to his special friends. He'll tax your harvests and vintage to support his expensive bureaucracy... He'll lay a tax on your flocks and you'll end up no better than slaves. The day will come when you will cry out in desperation because of this king you so much want for yourselves. But don't expect God to answer."* (1Sa 8:10-18 MSG)

The people were obstinate and cried out, "We want a king, we want a king! We want a king to lead us in battle just like other countries."

So, against my wishes and because the Lord had consented to the people's request, I began searching for a worthy candidate. One morning, shortly after sunrise, as I was in prayer, the Lord spoke to me and said that the next day I would see a young man from the tribe of Benjamin. It was he I was to anoint as king.

Sure enough, the next morning I met this handsome tall youth in the gateway of the town, and the Lord assured me this was the man.

The young man came up to me and asked, "Where can I find the seer? Maybe he can help me find my father's donkeys."

Let me explain that until recently it has been customary to call the prophet a seer, and people still come to me to seek guidance.

I responded by saying, "I am the seer," and then added, "I want you to eat with me today, and, by the way, your father's lost donkeys have been found."

That afternoon I had a sumptuous meal prepared. I invited about thirty guests and sat the young man, whose name I learned was Saul, and his servant at the head of the table. When the meal was served, I made sure that an exceptionally large and juicy steak was brought to Saul.

We talked late into the night on the roof of my house, and I got to know more about Saul and his family. The next morning, as I was walking with him on his way out of town, I told him to tell his servant to go on ahead of us because I had special message from God for him.

I took out a flask of olive oil and poured it on his head, kissed him, and said, "The Lord has anointed you king to rule over his people."

A few weeks later, I called an assembly of the people in Mizpah, but when I was going to present Saul to the people, I could not find him. He was hiding among the supplies people had brought. I finally got him to come out and introduced him to the crowd. He was a head taller than anyone else.

I said to the people: "Here is the man the Lord has chosen as king. There is no one else in Israel like him."

And the people burst out, exclaiming, "Long live King Saul! Long live the King!"

Though the excitement was contagious and spread over the country, I must confess that down in the depths of my soul, I wasn't too happy. I guess I felt slighted -- relegated to the sidelines. I suppose I should have been more supportive of our new king, but I wasn't.

Soon I began to see things that bothered me. On one occasion, when he was preparing to fight the Philistines near Gilgal, the outcome of the battle looked bleak. He didn't wait for me to get there to offer up the burnt offering to the Lord but went ahead and did it himself.

I was very upset. When I confronted him, he said, "The situation was precarious, and when I saw how many of my men were going AWOL, and how exposed we were to an attack by the Philistines, I suddenly realized

I had not asked the Lord for his help. I took matters in my own hands and decided to offer up the burnt offering myself."

Saul also began showing erratic behavior. I was told about an incident when he demanded that the soldiers take an oath prohibiting them from eating anything before evening. After the oath had been made, Jonathan who had been involved in routing a detachment of Philistine soldiers and was ignorant of the oath, saw a honeycomb and ate some. After the troops heard of this they began slaughtering some of the animals taken as plunder and eating the meat with the blood. When this was reported to Saul, he was incensed and vowed to punish by death anyone who had broken the oath. The lot fell to Jonathan, and his father ordered that he be killed. The troops, recognizing that the battle had been won because of Jonathan's bravery, rallied in his support and saved him.

And finally, there was the incident after the victory over the Amalekites. Even though the Lord had clearly instructed me to tell Saul to destroy everything, he took the sheep and cattle as spoils of war.

I came to realize that this man, who had come from humble origins in the backwoods of the smallest of the tribes, the tribe of Benjamin, and once had been so timid he shied away from becoming king, was now swollen with his own importance. Instead of humbly following the Lord, he was determined to have his own way.

One day, the Lord spoke to me and said, "So how long are you going to mope over Saul. You know I've rejected him as king over Israel. Fill your flask with anointing oil and get going. I'm sending you to Jesse of Bethlehem. I've spotted the very king I want among his sons." (1Sa 16:1 MSG) Then he added, "He is a young man after my own heart."

So I went to Bethlehem, called the elders of the town together, and prepared a sacrifice to the Lord. When Jesse and his sons arrived, I was about to anoint the oldest as king, but the Lord restrained me saying, "The Lord does not look at the things people look at. People look at the outward appearance, but the Lord looks at the heart." (1Sa16:7)

Jesse called six more of his sons to appear before me, but I did not sense the Lord had chosen any one of them, so I asked him, "Are these all your sons?"

He replied, "I have one more. He's out in the fields taking care of the sheep."

"Send for him," I said.

When he arrived, I saw a handsome young man full of health and vigor. I felt the Lord saying to me, "This is my man, anoint him."

A doubt crept into my mind -- I thought the Lord did not look on outward appearances...but I sensed it was wiser not to question him about this.

So I took the flask of oil and anointed David in the presence of his brothers and the elders. From that day on the Spirit of Lord came upon him for he was a man after the Lord's own heart.

7

THE WOMAN WHO
DEFUSED VIOLENCE

1 Samuel 25

I decided to join David's band of what you could call "guerilla warriors" while he was hiding from Saul. We found refuge in the Judean Wilderness but had to keep wandering from place to place. Sometimes we made alliances with local leaders for protection. It was scary business, and we were often in need of supplies and food.

On one occasion, when we were camped in the Desert of Paran, a large flock of sheep was grazing nearby, and we became friends with the shepherds who were watching over them. Because there were bands of marauding bandits, we offered the shepherds our protection.

In a conversation I struck up with one them, I asked, "Who is the owner of this flock?"

"Nabal. He lives near Carmel," he replied curtly.

I commented, "Your master must be a very wealthy man."

"He is," the shepherd replied and then added, "he has three thousand sheep and one thousand goats."

"The Lord has really blessed him," I said.

"Perhaps that is so, but…" he hesitated and then said in contempt, "he is a self-centered, arrogant, brute."

"Why do you say that?" I asked, surprised at this response.

"I'd rather not go into details," the man said.

With this strange answer, I decided to drop the matter and shifted to light talk about the healthy condition of the sheep.

At harvest festival time, we learned that Nabal was shearing some of his sheep and might have a big cookout, so David decided to send a delegation to Carmel and see if Nabal would be willing to share some of the food with us.

He chose me to take nine other men and go to Nabal with the following message:

"Peace and the blessings of God upon you and all your household! We have heard that you are shearing your sheep and will celebrate with a cook out. When your shepherds were camped near us, we protected them and the flock from the roving cattle rustlers. You can ask one of your men how we treated them. As a favor, I am asking you to be generous with my men, give whatever you can to them, for they and I are your faithful servants."

When we located Nabal, we gave him David's message and waited for an answer. Nabal began strutting back and forth in front of his tent, and then, shouting in anger and contempt, he said, "Who is this David character? I don't know him nor his father. I don't even know where you guys are from. These days the country is full of runaway servants and slaves. You men might be some of them. If you think I'm going to take our wine, the bread our women baked, and the fresh meat we grilled for our sheepshearers who have worked hard, and give it to men I have never seen before, you're badly mistaken."

We got the message and decided to clear out as fast as we could. When we got back to camp, I reported to David how Nabal had received us. He was incensed and said, "We'll show that brute a thing or two. Strap on your swords and let's go after him."

David started off with four hundred men, leaving two hundred to guard the camp. As I was riding along beside him, he said to me, "*That sure was a waste, guarding everything this man had out in the wild so that nothing he had was lost -- and now he rewards me with insults. A real slap in the face! May God do his worst to me if Nabal and every cur in his misbegotten brood aren't dead meat by morning."* (1Sa 25:21-22 MSG)

As we rode down into a ravine, we saw a caravan coming towards us. When it drew near, this beautiful and elegantly dressed woman got off her donkey, rushed up to David, bowed reverently, threw herself at his feet, and said, "Please pardon me, your humble servant, for my presumption. I plead with you to hear what I have to say."

David snapped, "Go ahead, but make it fast. I am on an important mission and in a hurry."

She then said, "My name is Abigail, and I am Nabal's wife. I did not see the men you sent to the barbecue. One of our servants reported to me how my husband received them. Now I beg you not to consider his action, for his name means Fool. He has acted the part. Foolhardiness follows him everywhere. Now, dear sir, as surely as the Lord lives and you live, since God has preserved you from punishing my husband and avenging your honor by shedding his blood and the blood of his servants with your own hands, may all those intent on harming you be like Nabal."

She then had her servants unload the donkeys which were carrying two hundred loaves of bread, two skins of wine, five dressed sheep, five sacks of roasted grain, a hundred cakes of raisins, and two hundred cakes of pressed figs.

After the servants had finished unloading the donkeys, Abigail said to David, "May the Lord our God give you a lasting dynasty as you defend his name. While you fight the Lord's battles, he will keep you from evil and from those who wish to harm you. The Lord will bind up your life in a bundle of protection, and after God has given you every good thing he has promised you and installed you as king over Israel, you will not have on your conscience the burden of needless bloodshed. After the Lord has given you success, I ask you to remember me."

David responded by saying, "Praise the Lord God who sent you to meet me and stop me from what I intended to do. May you be blessed by the Lord for your courage and good judgment. You kept me from shedding blood and avenging myself. Otherwise, I would have harmed you, and I would have killed your husband and his men.

Then he took her hand, accepted all the gifts she offered him, and said, "Go home in peace. I have heard you and granted your request."

We later heard that when Abigail returned home, she found her husband holding a big party, almost like a royal party, and he was dead drunk. She didn't tell him what she had done until the next day when he was sober. When he heard her report, he flew into a rage, had a serious heart attack, and ten days later was dead.

After the news reached David that Nabal was dead, he commented, *"Blessed be God who has stood up for me against Nabal's insults, kept me from an evil act, and let Nabal's evil boomerang back on him."* (1Sa 25:39 MSG)

Sometime later, David confided in me that he was in love with Abigail. I was very pleased and told him I thought it would be wonderful if he married such a beautiful, intelligent and wise woman. He dispatched me and some other servants to Carmel, and I told Abigail that David had sent us to take her back with us to become his wife.

She didn't keep us waiting for an answer but instructed her five servants to pack her belongings. Then she got on her donkey, returned with us to our camp and became David's wife.

8

BATHSHEBA TELLS HER STORY

2 Samuel 11, 12, 1 Kings 1:9-35

I was born on the Sabbath and that is why my father Eliam gave me the name Bathsheba. He enlisted in the royal army of King David, and, as is customary in military families. we moved around a lot from garrison to garrison. After he had been promoted as an officer, he was finally stationed in Jerusalem, and I found it exciting to be in the big bustling city.

One evening my father brought a fellow officer to the house for supper. In the conversation around the table, we learned that Uriah was a Hittite, from a region to the far north, and that he had come to Jerusalem because of his interest in knowing more about our religion. He had offered his services as a mercenary in the royal army.

Uriah visited our home frequently and began showing an interest in me. I looked forward to his visits, and one night, some months after the first visit, he asked my father if he could marry me. I was thrilled, for I was in love with him and had always dreamed of marrying an officer of the royal army for the prestige that went with it. My parents were hesitant to grant his wish because he was not a Jew. With his persistence and my love for him, we finally got my parents' permission and were married.

After my husband was assigned to the royal guard, we found a small house near the palace. I was happy the first few years of our marriage, but then my husband was deployed to fight King David's battles against the Philistines, Moabites, Edomites and others. He began spending more time away at war than at home. I was lonely and felt depressed much of the time.

And, when he was home, he could never leave his military discipline and authority outside but issued orders as if on the field. He relived the battles, was disturbed at night by his dreams, and shared with me many of the gruesome details of his encounters.

Even though we desperately wanted a child, I could not conceive, and this was a source of pain and shame for me and great disappointment for my husband.

One spring afternoon when winter had bid us farewell, the leaves on the olive trees were arriving to greet us, and my husband was away at war, I decided to take my bath in the patio of our house and enjoy the warm sunshine. I undressed and began bathing when I noticed a man on the roof of the royal palace gazing at me. I was embarrassed, quickly covered myself, and went inside. This incident disturbed me. I could not explain the strange feelings that seemed to surface and the thoughts they triggered.

A few days later some men knocked at the door of our house and handed me a note. It was an invitation to have supper with King David at the royal palace, and the messengers wanted an immediate reply. I was taken aback. Why would the King want me, a humble woman, to come to the palace? Then it dawned on me that the man who had seen me taking my bath was the King. Conflicting thoughts flew into my mind -- some like beautiful butterflies and others like African bees. What should I do? Could it be that a man, not just any man, but the King, wanted me? I hesitated, but finally told the men I would accept the invitation.

That afternoon I bathed, sprinkled on the best perfumes, and carefully chose my outfit. I put on the gold necklace and earrings that Uriah had brought me as bounty from the battle for the city of Damascus and walked over to the palace.

The King's personal secretary received me and ushered me into the reception room. I was in awe -- the tapestries on the wall, the designs on the stone floor and the gold candelabras were beautiful. A half hour later King David appeared, dressed in his finest robes, and escorted me into the dining room where the palace servants served us a sumptuous feast of grilled fish, raisin and fig cakes and plenty of good wine.

The conversation around the table was pleasant. The King talked about the various military campaigns and inquired about my husband. I could tell he was pleased to have me there. I was so excited by his attention and by being with such an important person that I had trouble containing myself. After supper he invited me into his bed chamber. Because I felt the need for intimacy, I could not resist the affectionate overtures of someone so important and powerful. Even though I was still in the purification period of seven days after my menstrual cycle, I surrendered to his advances.

The next morning, after I had arrived back at my house, a dark cloud of guilt and shame came over me which I could not dispel. Warring thoughts and feelings fought in my mind. How could I have done such a thing? How could I have been unfaithful to my husband? Was my need for intimacy satisfied by this one-night stand? The following weeks were so torturous I seldom ventured out of the house.

When I discovered I was pregnant, my shame was overshadowed by the hope and excitement of having my first child. I sent a note to the King. He replied by telling me to be patient.

Two weeks later my husband arrived in town. After reporting to the King, he came by the house briefly to tell me he would spent the night at the palace garrison, because he felt that since his commander Joab and all the troops were camped out in tents, it would not be fitting for him to have the luxury of sleeping comfortably at home with his wife. I could not gather enough courage to reveal to him what had happened, and, even if I had, he didn't give me enough time to do so. Two days later he came by to tell me that he was returning to the battle against the Ammonites. I was saddened but relieved.

About a month later, a soldier came to the house and handed me a note from the King which informed me that my husband had been killed in the siege of the city of Rabah. The note also said that, after my period of mourning, he, the King, would send messengers to take me to the palace to be his wife. I closed the door and flung myself on the couch, completely distraught. For a few days I grieved over the loss of my husband, but a narrow beam of light began to break through the dark cloud of guilt and shame --the excitement over the prospect of becoming King David's wife and having a baby.

One day while I was still in mourning, my father came by to see how I was getting along. Both he and my husband, Uriah, were members of a cohort of thirty brave men that were assigned especially dangerous work (2Sa 23:34, 39). He told me he had requested a special home leave, so he could come and share with me some details of my husband's death. I could tell my father was troubled. While we were having supper he shared the following with me:

"Our cohort laid siege to the city of Rabah. As we approached the walls of the city, some Ammonite soldiers came out from the gate and attacked us. But we were able to drive them back. Then suddenly our soldiers retreated and left Uriah and me exposed. The Ammonite archers on the wall took advantage of this and shot a volley of arrows. One hit Uriah and he was killed, but I survived because I hid behind a rock. Later I was able to get back to our camp. I was upset by the failure of our troops to support us, and that evening, as we sat around the campfire, I asked the officer in charge of the attack what had led to the retreat of our troops. He took me aside and told me that he had received an order from Joab the commander, to retreat and leave Uriah and me exposed.

"I was shocked. So the next day I sought out Joab and asked him why he had given that strange order, which put Uriah and me in critical danger. He showed me a note from King David with the precise order to back away from Uriah so he would be killed."

I sat in silence for a long time trying to digest what my father had shared. What a crazy, mixed-up world we live in -- adultery, infidelity, deceit and even murder on the one hand, but also courage and loyalty on the other. I wondered how I could navigate through all this.

At the end of my mourning, I became King David's wife. The loneliness and confusion slowly receded as I focused my attention on my new husband and the child we were expecting, and I began to savor the intimacy I had so longed for but had never experienced before.

The months went by swiftly, and I gave birth to a beautiful baby boy. David and I were ecstatic. Some days later, while we were having breakfast, a servant came and informed David that the prophet Nathan wanted to see him.

I asked David, "Who is this Nathan?"

"He is a prophet who has given me messages from the Lord at various times," he replied, and with this he got up and left the room.

About an hour later, while I was on our bed nursing the baby, David returned visibly shaken. His voice trembled as he said:

"Nathan told me about a certain rich man who had a large flock of sheep and a herd of cattle, and a poor man who lived nearby. He farmed the rich man's land and had only one little ewe lamb he had purchased. He raised it, his children played with it, it even ate from his table, and slept in his arms. It was like a little daughter to him.

| "A traveler came to visit the rich man. The rich man refrained from slaughtering one of his own animals to prepare a meal for his guest. Instead he took the little lamb that belonged to the poor man and had it slaughtered and prepared for his guest.

"I was so upset by this that I immediately determined to have the rich man punished and make him pay four times for the lamb…"

David clenched his fists and dropped to the floor sobbing.

"What's wrong?" I asked.

In the midst of his sobs, he blurted out, "Nathan pointed his finger at me, and said 'You're the man.' Then he went on and said, 'The Lord anointed you king over Israel and delivered you from the attacks of Saul giving you his household. He gave you all Judah and Israel. And, if all this were not sufficient, he would have given you more. Why did you walk away from the word of the Lord by having Uriah killed and taking his wife? You committed adultery and murder.'"

Then David said, "I threw myself at Nathan's feet and cried out: 'I have sinned against the Lord!' Nathan lifted me up and said that because of his mercy, the Lord would forgive me."

When I heard these words, I wondered if the Lord would forgive me for my infidelity.

Then David added dejectedly, "But Nathan said that the baby would die."

I cried out, "Why should an innocent child die on account of the sins of his parents?"

David didn't answer me, he just took me in his arms, and together we wept.

The baby took sick. Even though David fasted, spent the nights wrapped in sackcloth, pled with God for the child, and I joined him in prayer, our little son grew progressively weaker. Seven days later he died. David tried to comfort me, but I was disconsolate and never really recovered from the loss until the birth of our second son, Solomon.

One day when I was buried in my grief and guilt, I happened to stumble on a scroll where my husband jots down his musings and poems and found these verses:

> *My guilt has overwhelmed me*
> *like a burden too heavy to bear.*
> *I am bowed down and brought very low;*
> *all day long I go about mourning.*
> *All my longings lie open before you, Lord;*
> *my sighing is not hidden from you.*
> (Ps 38:4, 6, 9)

Then further down I read:

> *When I kept silent, my bones wasted away*
> *through my groaning all day long.*
> *Then I acknowledged my sin to you*
> *and did not cover up my iniquity.*
> *I said, "I will confess my transgressions to the Lord."*
> *And you forgave the guilt of my sin.*
> (Ps 32:3, 5)

I knelt by my bed, poured out my heart to the Lord, and kept repeating these words which were like balm to my troubled soul until they penetrated the deepest recesses of my spirit.

I sat on the bed, unrolled the scroll further and found these words:

> *I waited patiently for the Lord;*
> *he turned to me and heard my cry.*
> *he lifted me out of the slimy pit,*
> *out of the mud and mire;*
> *and set my feet on a rock*
> *and gave me a firm place to stand.*
> *He put a new song in my mouth,*
> *a hymn of praise to our God.*
> (Ps 40:1-3)

I took scroll, put it in its place, and that night I slept peacefully for the first time in months.

9

THE CONTEST ON MOUNT CARMEL

1 Kings 18 and 21

My name is Obadiah and I have been a faithful follower of the God of Israel all my life. I am greatly distressed to see how our nation has drifted away from the Lord since our first king Jeroboam separated from the Kingdom of Judah seventy-five years ago and rebelled against God. He was afraid the people would continue going to Jerusalem to worship at the temple of Solomon, so he established two sanctuaries --one in the north at Dan and the other in the south at Bethel. He placed a golden calf in each one for the people to worship.

When Ahab became king of Israel, I thought I could be a positive influence in his life by offering my services as his palace administrator, but it has been almost impossible to stem the tide of idolatry and corruption.

Ahab married Jezebel, the daughter of Ethbaal king of Sidon, and she has compounded the idolatry by introducing the worship of the pagan god Baal. Ahab built a temple to Baal in our capital city of Samaria to please his wife and erected a pole to honor Asherah, one of the Canaanite goddesses. When Jezebel began rounding up and killing off the prophets of the Lord, I knew I had to take action, so I hid one hundred of them in two caves, fifty in each, and provided them with food and water.

To illustrate the wickedness of this royal couple, I must tell you of an incident that occurred. Ahab wanted to grow a vegetable garden. The vineyard that his neighbor Naboth owned near the palace was the perfect spot, for it had an adequate supply of water. The king offered to buy the vineyard or exchange it for a better one, but Naboth refused because the property had been in his family for generations.

Ahab was so upset by Naboth's refusal that when he returned to Samaria, he went to bed sulking and refused to eat. Jezebel observed his sullen attitude and asked him what was the matter. Ahab told her that Naboth had refused to part with his vineyard.

I can still hear her shrill voice as she responded, "Is this any way for the king of Israel to behave? Come on now. Cheer up, for I will get the vineyard of this Naboth character for you."

I saw her sit down at a table and write a letter which she stamped with the king's official seal, call a servant, and instruct him to take the letter to the elders of Jezreel. Later I learned from one of the elders the contents of the letter. She instructed them to proclaim a day of fasting, to seat Naboth in a prominent place, and have two scoundrels sitting in front of him charge him with blaspheming God and cursing the king, and, finally, take him out and stone him.

When she received the report that the lynching had taken place, she told her husband that Naboth was dead, and he could go down to Jezreel and take possession of the vineyard. This is only one example of the corruption at the highest levels of our government.

Because the situation is so desperate, God has raised up an extraordinary prophet by the name of Elijah from the village of Tishbe, in the region of Gilead, to proclaim the Lord's judgment on the nation and show forth his power.

Elijah inaugurated his ministry with a scary prophecy. He told King Ahab that there would be no rain nor dew until he, Elijah, asked the Lord to lift the curse. Three years into the drought, when the grazing lands were dry as a bone, crops had failed, and the lack of food was severe in Samaria, Ahab said we should go through the land searching in the valleys for grass to keep the animals alive. He would go one way and I the other. I started out, and a few days later, as I was walking along, I met Elijah.

He said to me, "Go tell King Ahab that I am here."

I immediately replied, "The king has sent his servants to look for you everywhere. He has even sent emissaries to neighboring countries and made their kings swear they are not hiding you. If I tell him you are here, and then if the Spirit of the Lord leads you somewhere else and the king does not find you, he will put me to death."

Elijah promised me he would not disappear, so I informed the king of his whereabouts. Ahab came, walked up to Elijah, and said in a defiant voice, "Is that you, the troublemaker of Israel?"

Elijah looked him in the eye and said, "You are the troublemaker. You have abandoned the Lord God and have served the Baals. Now summon the four hundred fifty prophets of Baal and the four hundred prophets of Asherah who eat at Jezebel's table every day and send messengers all over Israel to call the people. Let us all gather on Mount Carmel where we will see who is God over Israel."

I accompanied King Ahab, and early on the appointed day, we gathered on Mount Carmel. Elijah addressed the crowd in a loud, strong voice, "Get two bulls. The prophets of Baal will choose one, cut it into pieces, put it on the wood pyre, but do not light the fire. I will prepare the other bull the same way but will not set it on fire. Then you all will call on the name your god, and I will call on the name of the Lord. The one who answers by fire... he is God."

The prophets of Baal took one of the bulls, prepared it, and called on the name of Baal. They danced around the altar until noon, but there was no response. Elijah began to mock them, *"Pray louder! He is a god! Maybe he is day-dreaming or relieving himself, or perhaps he's gone off on a trip! Or maybe he's sleeping and you've got to wake him up!"* (1 Kg 18.27 TEV)

So the prophets prayed with loud cries, dancing around frantically, cutting themselves with knives and swords until they were covered with blood. This went on until time for the evening sacrifice, but no one answered.

Elijah then prepared the other bull, took twelve stones -- one for each of the tribes descended from Jacob, rebuilt the Lord's altar, dug a trench around it, arranged the wood, and placed the pieces of the bull on the altar. He then instructed the men to fill four large stone jars with water and pour the water on the altar. He told them to refill the jars and pour the water on the altar again, and, when they did it a third time, the water even ran into the trench and filled it.

At the time for the evening sacrifice, Elijah drew near the altar, lifted his arms, and began praying in a firm reverent voice, "*Lord, the God of Abraham, Isaac and Israel, let it be known today that you are God in Israel and that I am your servant and have done all these things at your command. Answer me, Lord, answer me, so these people will know that you are God, and that you are turning their hearts back again.*" (1 Ki 18:36, 37)

There was a loud thunder clap and a stream of fire came down from the sky and incinerated the sacrifice, the wood, the stones, and swallowed up the water in the trench. When the people saw this, they fell prostrate and cried, "*The Lord is God -- he is God! The Lord -- he is God!* (1 Ki 18:39)

Elijah had the prophets of Baal rounded up, taken to the Kishon Valley, and killed. Then he instructed Ahab to go get a bite to eat before the rain came. Elijah remained on Mount Carmel with his head between his knees in worship before the Lord. Six times he told his servant to check the eastern sky, and each time the servant reported that he could see nothing. The seventh time the servant saw a small cloud rising from the sea. Then Elijah told the servant to go and tell Ahab to hitch up his chariot and go down before the rain flooded the road.

The sky darkened. The wind picked up and was soon howling and bending the trees. Big drops of rain splattered on the dusty road, and I smelled the odor of fresh rain on parched soil. The heavens opened up and the rain came down in buckets.

10

THE STILL SMALL VOICE OF GOD

1 Kings 19

Obadiah has reported on the corrupt situation in Israel under the reign of King Ahab and his wife Jezebel. He also described the amazing victory of God over the prophets of Baal in the contest on Mount Carmel, using me, Elijah, as his instrument, but I must tell you what happened after that. Even though it is embarrassing and shameful, it opened the door to a blessing from God.

I am sitting in the shade of a juniper tree in front of my hut one morning, reflecting joyously over what happened on Mount Carmel, when a man runs up to me, hands me a note with the king's seal on it, and hurries away as fast as he has come. I break the seal and read the note, "Baal is thirsting for revenge. Tomorrow by this time you will be as dead as the prophets you killed, and your carcass will be offered up to Baal. Queen Jezebel." Trembling, I read the note a second time.

A horrible emptiness grips my stomach, my heart races, and I find it hard to breathe. Fear controls my thoughts and terror grips me. I know what the queen is not only capable of doing but what she will do! I forget to call on the Lord who has always guided and protected me and decide to run for it. That very morning my servant and I flee south, and a few days later we reach Beersheba in Judah, about one hundred fifty miles from Jezreel.

I leave my servant there and go into the wilderness a day's journey, where I sit down under a broom brush. I lift my heart to the Lord in prayer, "I have had enough, Lord. Take my life, and let me join those who have gone before me."

Exhausted, I stretch out and fall asleep. Suddenly, someone touches me. I awake startled and see an angel who tells me to eat, and there, by my head, I find a jar of water and some fresh bread.

I lie down and sleep again. A second time the angel touches me and says, "Get up and eat." Then he adds, "You've got a long journey ahead."

Strengthened by what the Lord has provided, I start out on a forty day trek to Mount Horeb, the mountain of God, in the wilderness of Sinai. On the way, the cloud of fear that has darkened my heart and mind begins to lift. Since I have never been this way before, everything is new: the barren landscape, the lofty mountains, the dry rocky gullies, the juniper trees, the various cactus plants, and the prickly pears, some of which are in bloom and others beginning to bear fruit. As I continue south, I pluck some of this delicious fruit which tastes sweeter each day. I recall how God had ravens feed me during the drought, while I was in the Brook Cherith, and how he provided for the widow of Zarephath, so she could supply me with food. Now, I feast on his provision for me on my journey through this desert. I recall the victory of God over the prophets of Baal on Mount Carmel, and my soul revives. But I wonder, is God really directing my paths? Will he preserve my life?

Finally, I reach a plateau, and there in the distance I see Mount Horeb rising abruptly from the plain. As I walk slowly toward the enormous monolith with its barren rocky crevices, my mind goes back to the day, many years ago, when Moses and the children of Israel stood before this same mountain. It must have been a fearful sight to see the clouds of smoke billowing and the flames of fire erupting as from a volcano -- a sight much more fearful than the fire that came down and lit the altar on

Mount Carmel. A reverent fear comes over me as I realize the importance of this mountain in the history of my nation.

It is on this mountain that God spoke with Moses and gave him the law which has been the foundation of our society. And then I recall that while God was speaking with Moses and giving him the tablets of the law, down on the plain, perhaps exactly where I am now walking, Aaron collected the people's jewelry and made a golden calf for them to worship. Even though the first two commandments the Lord gave are clear, "You shall have no other gods before me and you shall not make for yourself an image in the form of anything in heaven, or on the earth, or in the waters below," many of our rulers have promoted idolatry and have committed terrible injustices. Today, with a pagan queen calling the shots, it is even worse. I cry out to the Lord, "O Lord, have mercy on your people."

I start the arduous climb, stumbling over rocks, skirting the edge of deep ravines, and about three-quarters of the way up, I come to a cave. Since my legs can't carry me any further, I crawl in, find a smooth spot, and fall fast asleep.

The sun is already climbing over the distant peaks when I hear the Lord asking, "What are you doing here, Elijah?"

I'm too ashamed to tell him I am here because I have been afraid of a wicked woman who is out to get me, so I divert the conversation and say, "Look, Lord, I have been very zealous for you, the Lord Almighty, and the people have not kept the promises they made to you. They have destroyed your altars and killed your priests." And then I add mournfully, "I'm the only one left, and they want to kill me, too."

After a long pause, I hear his answer, "Get out there. Stand in front of the mouth of the cave, and I will pass by you."

I do as instructed, and a powerful tornado sweeps over the plain below, hits the side of the mountain, and shatters the rocks. I fully expect to see the Lord, but he is not in the wind.

Then the whole earth begins to shake. Some of the big boulders are dislodged and go crashing down. I fall to the ground and hold on to a rock to keep from slipping over the precipice. I don't sense the presence of the Lord.

Fire rages around the mountain, and the flames creep up to where I am. I have to crawl into the cave. But the Lord is not in the fire.

After the flames die down, I go out and stand at the mouth of the cave. I cover my head with my cloak and look out over the plain. Everything is perfectly still, not even a breeze. A strange silence has come over the whole land, a silence like I have never experienced before. Two eagles I had seen circling over the mountain as I hiked up yesterday are perched on an outcropping above me, perfectly still. A lizard has come out from under a rock and stands motionless with his head cocked as though trying to listen. The silence has its own sound, the sound of sheer silence.

And then I hear a gentle murmur, like a soft whisper, a still small voice. It is the gentle voice of God who asks again, "Elijah, what are you doing here?"

All I can do is repeat what I said before, "Lord, I have been very zealous for you, and the people have not kept your law. They have destroyed your altars and killed your priests, and they want to kill me, too."

The Lord then says, "I want you to go back the way you came through the wilderness to the city of Damascus and anoint Hazael king over the Arameans, anoint Jehu king over Israel, and anoint Elisha to take your place as the prophet of the Lord."

If Jezebel was upset over the victory of God at Mount Carmel, can you imagine how she will react when I anoint Jehu as king in place of her husband Ahab? It will be like climbing out of the frying pan and dropping into the fire. I hesitate, weigh the options, and finally decide to obey the command. Empowered by the authority of the Lord, I go back the way I have come, pick up my servant in Beersheba, and then go on to the town of Abel Meholah to look for Elisha. I find him plowing his fields at the head of twelve yoke of oxen. I go up to him and cover him with my cloak. He understands this gesture as the call of God, slaughters his oxen, and roasts the meat over the fire of his burning plow. He celebrates with a big party for the people, kisses his parents good-bye, and becomes my apprentice.

But upon reaching Samaria, I learn that Ben-Hadad, the king of the Arameans, has sent messengers to King Ahab demanding tribute money, and war is about the break out. It seems to me that this is not a propitious time to anoint either Hazael or Jehu, so I leave this for Elisha to do later. Strictly speaking, this is not what the Lord instructed me to do. I hope he is not displeased with my decision.

11

TRUTH AND CONSEQUENCES

1 Kings 22

After three years of peace between Israel and Aram, King Ahab pointed out to his officials that the king of Aram had violated the treaty with Israel and had conquered Ramoth-gilead. When Jehoshaphat, king of the southern kingdom of Judah, paid King Ahab a visit, Ahab requested his military support to retake Ramoth-gilead. I was one of Ahab's officials so I can tell you what transpired.

Jehoshaphat pledged his support saying, "Yes sir, my soldiers and their horses will gladly fight alongside yours," but then he added, "First, I think we ought to consult the Lord for his guidance."

Since King Ahab does not really follow the God of Israel, I was surprised he agreed to call for an assembly of the prophets. When they arrived, I discovered that they were a mixed bag. Some of them claimed allegiance to the Lord God of Israel, and others who were clearly followers of Baal.

Ahab asked them what their opinion was, and in a unanimous chorus they shouted out, "God wants Ramoth-gilead back in Israel. Go get it! He will give you a swift victory."

King Jehoshaphat was clearly not pleased with this and he asked, "Is there not another prophet of God we might consult on this matter?"

King Ahab was bothered by this. He said in a sarcastic tone, "Well, if you insist, yes, there is another prophet, but I can't stand him for he never prophesies anything good for me, only bad things. His name is Micaiah, the son of Imlah."

"You shouldn't talk about a prophet of the Lord like that. Send for him."

Ahab called one of his junior officers and ordered, "Go immediately, get Micaiah and bring him to us.

The kings were arrayed in their royal robes, seated on their thrones in front of the gates of the capital city of Samaria. The prophets were putting on quite a show for the benefit of the whole crowd gathered there.

One of them, Zedekiah, had even made a set of horns, and brandishing them before the kings screamed out, "This is God's word. With these horns you will gore King Ben-Hadad of Aram, and there won't be anything left of him."

All the prophets joined in, "You're right! Ramoth-gilead will be an easy plum to pick from Aram's tree, a present for King Ahab."

When the junior officer returned with Micaiah, he presented the prophet to the king who said, "Micaiah, tell me, should we go to war and get Ramoth-gilead, or should we wait for a while?"

"Go ahead, lead the army to victory. It will be a gift from God," replied Micaiah sneeringly.

"Wait a minute," said the king. "Haven't I told you many times to tell me the truth, nothing but the truth." (*The Message*) And then he added, "Come on now, out with it!"

"OK," said the prophet. "You asked for it. I see all the people of Israel scattered over the hills like sheep without a shepherd. They will have no one to lead them, so they'll be clueless as to what to do."

Turning to Jehoshaphat, King Ahab said, "Didn't I tell you! He never has a good word from the Lord, only doom and destruction."

Micaiah continued, "I've got more to tell you. In a dream I saw the Lord sitting on his throne with all the hosts of heaven around him. And the Lord said, 'Who will go and deceive Ahab into attacking Ramoth-gilead and go to his death?' One of his servants suggested one thing and another something else. Finally, one stepped forward and said, 'I will go and deceive him.'

"The Lord said to him, 'How will you do it?'"

"'I will go and be a deceiving spirit in the minds of all the prophets.'"

"'You will succeed, so go do it.'"

"So the Lord has put deceit in the mouths of all these prophets, and disaster for you."

At this, Zedekiah ran up to Micaiah, slapped him on, the face and said, "Tell me, how is it that the Spirit of the Lord left me to go to you?

And Micaiah replied, "Wait until you are desperately looking for a place to hide."

"Enough of this," said Ahab. "Get this man out of here. Take him to the city magistrate and have him locked up. Don't give him anything but bread and water until I get back."

"If you ever get back safe and sound, I am no prophet of the living God," said Micaiah, and then added, "O people don't forget these words."

The kings went out to battle.

Ahab said to Jehoshaphat, "In preparation for the battle I will disguise myself, but you wear your royal apparel."

King Ben-Hadad of the Arameans had instructed his chariot commanders to locate Ahab and pursue him, so when they saw Jehoshaphat, they surmised that this was Ahab and they attacked him. When he cried out, they realized that he was not the king of Israel and stopped chasing him.

A flying arrow, shot at random, penetrated between Ahab's plates of armor. He immediately ordered his chariot driver to get him out of the thick of battle. On the sidelines, propped up in his chariot, with blood streaming from his wound, Ahab valiantly directed his troops, until he died just before sunset.

We brought his body back to Samaria and buried him. The soldiers washed the chariot at the pool where the prostitutes bathe, and the dogs licked his blood as the prophet Elijah had predicted.

And the chronicler of the kingdom wrote these words, "There was never anyone like Ahab, who sold himself to do evil in the eyes of the Lord, urged on by Jezebel his wife." (1 Kgs 21:25)

12

GREED HAS A PRICE

2 Kings 5

My name is Gehazi, and it has been my privilege to serve Elisha, the prophet, since he took up the cloak of his predecessor, Elijah, some years ago. I have seen, first-hand, the many ways God has revealed himself through this amazing man of God in these turbulent times. Our leaders and the people have abandoned the worship of the true God and have followed the pagan gods introduced by Jezebel and her puppet husband, King Ahab. I have tried to be responsible in the various tasks Elisha has asked me to carry out, but sometimes I have failed. Let me share one incident with you.

During these difficult years the kingdom of Israel has had numerous conflicts with the kingdom of Aram, but we have also had some peculiar exchanges. Naaman was a four star general, commander of the Aramean army. He was a courageous soldier, and his master, King Ben-Hadad, had great confidence in him because he had led the army to victory in many battles. But he was afflicted with a serious skin disease which may have been leprosy.

In one of his raids into Israel, his soldiers had taken captive a young Israelite girl who became the slave of Naaman's wife. When this girl learned that the general had this terrible disease, she confided in her mistress that there was a prophet in Israel who could cure her husband. The general's wife did not hesitate to share the information with her husband, and, since he was desperate, he dashed off to tell the king what the servant girl had suggested and get permission to come to Israel.

King Ben-Hadad offered to send a letter to King Joram of Israel. The letter read as follows, "With this letter I am sending my servant Naaman to you so that you may cure him of his leprosy."

Naaman took plenty of silver and gold and ten sets of expensive clothes and took off for Samaria. Upon his arrival he presented the letter to King Joram, who, when he read it, tore his robes in anger and confusion. King Joram said, "Am I God to take away life and bring it back again? Why does King Ben-Hadad send me his chief general to cure him of his skin disease?" He paused and then added, "What he is trying to do is create an international incident as an excuse to go to war."

As this was taking place in the king's palace, one of the servants hurried to inform my master Elisha who immediately sent me to the king with this message, "Why do you tear your robes in despair? Send the general to me, and he will see that there is a prophet of the Lord in Israel."

Naaman gathered his horses and chariots and followed me to Elisha's place. We stopped outside the door of the house. I went in and found Elisha sitting calmly at his table enjoying some fig cakes. When I informed him that the general was outside waiting for him, you would have thought that I told him a beggar wanted a handout.

He simply said, "Tell him to go wash seven times in the Jordan River. He will be cleansed and healed from his disease."

I knew this was not an appropriate way to receive an important person like General Naaman and feared the consequences, but I went out and told the general what Elisha had said.

Sure enough, Naaman blew his top and said in anger, "Doesn't he realize who I am? At least he could have come out and greeted me personally, could have called on the name of his God, maybe even waved his hand as a sign over the red spots, and pronounced the words, 'Be cleansed.' The rivers of Abana and Pharpar near Damascus are cleaner than your muddy little stream. I could at least have bathed in them."

He turned and stormed off in a huff.

His servants ran after him, and, when they caught up to him, said, "If the prophet had told you to do something courageous and important, wouldn't you have done it? Since he instructed you to do something so simple as going down to the Jordan and washing yourself, why don't you do it?"

They finally convinced him, so he went down to the Jordan, dipped in the water seven times, and slowly the natural tan color returned to his skin. His flesh was cleansed and became like that of a youth, and his heart burst with joy and gratitude. He and his servants traveled the twenty miles back to Samaria. He found Elisha, and he said to my master, "I am now convinced, like I have never been convinced before, that there is no other god in all the earth like the God of Israel. In gratitude for what you have done for me, please accept a gift."

"Sorry," replied Elisha, "but as surely as the God I serve lives, I will not accept a thing from you. I do not serve God for gain."

Naaman insisted, but he could not persuade Elisha, so he said, "Since you will not accept a gift from me, then I have a request to make."

"What is it?" asked Elisha.

"Let me take as much dirt and gravel as a couple of mules can carry. This will be a reminder that in this land I found the true God, and I will never offer a sacrifice to any other god."

"That's fine with me," affirmed Elisha.

Naaman added, "But may the Lord forgive me for this one thing. When my master King Ben-Hadad enters the temple of the god Rimmon and bows down to worship, since he will be leaning on my arm, I will also have to bow down. When I do this, may the Lord forgive me for this act."

"The peace of the Lord go with you," said Elisha.

This is where I come into the picture. When Naaman had been gone about two hours, a thought crept quietly into my head, "My master has let this Aramean Naaman slip through his fingers without so much as a thank you. By the living God, I'm going after him to get something or other from him." (2 Kgs 5:20 MSG)

So I took off, and, when I caught up to Naaman, he asked me, "What's up? Has something gone wrong?"

"No sir, everything is OK," I said. "Two young prophets have come to us from the hill country and they need help. Please give me seventy-five pounds of silver and two sets of clothes for them."

"I'll be glad to help. Take one hundred fifty pounds and two sets of clothes," replied Naaman.

He had his servants tie the silver and clothes in two bags and ordered two of them to help me carry them back. When I got to the hill near Elisha's house, I sent the servants back and hid the bags in a little fort there.

Elisha was waiting for me and asked, "What have you been up to, Gehazi?"

"*Nothing much,*" I answered. (2 Kgs 5:25 *MSG*)

Then Elisha, the man of God, said to me, "You should have known that my spirit was with you when the general got down from his chariot to greet you. Do you think this is the time to look out for yourself, line your pockets with gifts, and then cover up what you have done? You will now suffer from Naaman's skin disease."

That night the burning sensation on my back was so severe I couldn't sleep, and the next morning I saw all the color gone from my skin. It was a long time before it came back.

This shameful incident taught me that greed has its price.

13

GOD DELIVERS JERUSALEM

2 Kings 18 and 19

King Hezekiah instructed Eliakim, his palace administrator, Shebna, his royal secretary, and me, Joah, the court historian, to go to the aqueduct of the Upper Pool on the road to the Washerman's Field, just outside the city of Jerusalem. There we met with the emissaries of King Sennacherib: his commanding general, his deputy, and his field marshal. Stretched out behind them, we saw the Assyrian army with its siege ramps and other battle gear. It was an imposing and threatening sight!

For the past fifteen years we have been living under a dark cloud of fear --threatened by the expansionist policies of the Assyrian Empire. The Assyrian army conquered Damascus, the capital of Aram, and the Assyrian tentacles slowly began swallowing up the rest of the land. Four years after Hezekiah ascended to the throne of Judah, Shalmanezer, the new king of Assyria, attacked Samaria, the capital of Israel, our northern neighbor. After a devastating siege of three years during which many of its inhabitants died of starvation and disease, the city fell. Many people of the country were deported to Assyria, and foreigners were brought in to settle the land.

To us, here in Jerusalem, it was clear that God had brought this disaster upon our cousins in the north because they had abandoned the living God, were worshipping pagan gods, and were doing many detestable and wicked things. Even though the Lord sent prophets like Elijah and Amos to warn them, they had not repented but persisted in their evil ways.

It is true that some of our Judean kings have also forsaken God and the teachings of his law. For example, King Ahaz, who, when he went to Damascus to confer with the king of Assyria and saw the king's pagan altar, had a copy of it made to replace the altar of the Lord in the temple in Jerusalem. But Hezekiah has been a good king. He has tried to the clean up the mess he inherited from his father Ahaz. He has destroyed the pagan altars and the Asherah poles at which the people worshipped. He also broke in pieces the bronze snake that Moses made many years ago because the people had been burning incense to it. He has repaired the temple of the Lord and reinstituted the worship of the God of Israel. And, for the first time in many years, under his initiative we celebrated our national festivals of Unleavened Bread and Passover.

Since Hezekiah refused to pay tribute to the king of Assyria and led a conspiracy of other Palestinian nations against Assyria, he knew there would be consequences. He began strengthening the fortifications of Jerusalem and fortified the central cities of Judah. He ordered a tunnel dug through the rock to divert water from Gihon Spring, which lies outside the walls of the city of Jerusalem, to the pool of Siloam within the walls, thus securing the water supply for the city.

A short time ago we began receiving reports of the advance of the Assyrian forces along the Phoenician coast. They dethroned the king of Tyre, defeated the Egyptian army in the valley of Eltekeh, and, after conquering the Philistine cities of Ashkelon and Ekron, turned east towards Judah. Then couriers began arriving with news of the fall of Gath, Anathoth, and other towns in central Judah. From Lachish, the king of Assyria sent the delegation of officers and the army spread out before us, demanding the unconditional surrender of the land of Judah and our capital city, Jerusalem. Fear gripped me.

Their spokesman was the field marshal whose title, we learned, was Rabshakeh. He boomed loudly the message he claimed the king of Assyria had given him to tell Hezekiah, "'On whom have you depended to deliver you so that you rebelled against me. *You claim to have military strength, but the truth is that you have only toy soldiers. Are you trusting Egypt to defend you? Well, I've got news for you, Egypt is only a splintered reed of a staff, who pierces the hand of anyone who leans on it!* (2 Ki 18:21) You say you are trusting in your God. Didn't you remove the places of worship throughout the land for the people worship only in Jerusalem?"

The Rabshakeh continued broadcasting his message, "Come on, strike a deal with the great king of Assysria. You couldn't even put riders on two thousand horses if I gave them to you. You are depending on horses and chariots from Egypt, but you could not even repulse a junior officer from my army. And, what is more, the Lord God you worship, he himself has told me to conquer this city and destroy it."

Since the crowds of people on the city wall were listening and understanding his words, we said to him, "Please speak to us in Aramaic, for we understand it. Don't speak in Hebrew because the people will understand you."

He got red in the face and blurted out, "Do you think my master sent me to say these things only for the benefit of your king and not for the people on the wall? Your're wrong! They, like you, will have to eat their own excrement and drink their own urine."

And then he launched out in a loud tirade in Hebrew, "Hear the word of the mighty king of Assyria, and do not pay any attention to your midget king who is telling you to trust in the Lord God for deliverance. Make peace with me and you will be able to plant your own vineyards and drink water from your own cisterns until I come and take you to a new land filled with grain, vineyards, olive trees, and honey. I offer you life and not death! Hezekiah tells you to trust in the Lord for deliverance… Has any god delivered his people from the king of Assyria? What were the gods of all the Phoenician and Philistine cities doing when I conquered them? Did the gods rescue Damascus and Samaria? Don't be foolish. How can your god deliver Jerusalem from the hand of the great king of Assyria?"

The people listened in silence to this tirade while we tore our clothes and then rushed to report back to King Hezekiah. He, too, ripped his royal robes, put on a burlap sack, and went in to the temple of God. In desperation, he sent my companions, Eliakim and Shebna, along with senior priests to the prophet Isaiah with this message:

"This is a dark and fearful day of doom, like the day a baby is ready to be born, and its mother has no strength to deliver the child. Perhaps the Lord your God will hear the blasphemous words of the field marshal, whom the king of Assyria has sent to make fun of the living God, and the Lord will rebuke him. Pray for those of us who are left."

Isaiah sent this message, "Tell the king, The Lord says not to be afraid of what you have heard -- those blasphemous words from the mouth of the puppets of the king of Assyria. A rumor will trouble the king, and he will return to his own country where he will be killed."

When the field marshal received a report that King Sennacherib might have to engage an Ethiopian army, he left with part of the army to support the king.

Later, Sennacherib sent another envoy to Hezekiah with this message, *"Don't let that god that you think so much of keep stringing you along with the line, 'Jerusalem will never fall to the king of Assyria.' That's a barefaced lie. You know the track record of the kings of Assyria -- country after country laid waste, devastated. And what makes you think you'll be an exception? Take a good look at those wasted nations, destroyed by my ancestors; did their gods do them any good?"* (2 Ki 19:10-12 MSG)

Hezekiah read the message, returned to the temple of the Lord, spread the message out before the Lord, and prayed, "Lord, God of Israel, enthroned in the heavens, you are the only God, and you rule over all the nations of the earth. You created the heavens and the earth. Open your ears and listen to how Sennacherib has ridiculed you, and open your eyes and see how arrogant he is. It is true, O Lord, that the Assyrian kings have conquered nations and devastated the land. They have made bonfires of their gods, but they were only gods made of wood and stone and fashioned by human hands. O Lord, deliver us from the hand of the king of Assyria, *"so that all the kingdoms of the earth may know that you alone, Lord, are God."* (2 Ki 19:19)

While Hezekiah was pouring out his heart to God in prayer, Isaiah the prophet sent him another message: "The Lord God of Israel has heard your prayer, and this is my message to Sennacherib, the king of Assyria:

> 'You cursed shouted, and sneered at me the Holy God of Israel.
> You let your officials insult me, the Lord.
> And here is what you have said about yourself,
> I led my chariots to the highest heights of Lebanon's mountains.
> I went deep into its forest, cutting down the best cedar and cypress trees.
> I dried up every stream in the land of Egypt,
> and I drank water from wells I had dug.
> 'Sennacherib, now listen to me, the Lord,
> I planned all this long ago.
> And you don't even realize that I alone am the one who decided that you would do these things.
> I let you make ruins of fortified cities...
> I know all about you, even how fiercely angry you are with me.
> I have seen your pride and the tremendous hatred you have for me.
> Now I will put a hook in your nose, a bit in your mouth, then I will send you back to where you came from.
> 'Hezekiah..., I promise that the king of Assyria won't get to Jerusalem,
> or shoot an arrow into the city, or even surround it and prepare to attack.
> As surely as I am the Lord, he will return by the way he came
> and will never enter Jerusalem.
> I will protect it for myself and for my servant David' ".
>   (2 Ki 19:22-25, 27-29, 32-34 CEV)

That very night the angel of the Lord struck the camp of the Assyrian army with a plague, and the next morning the bodies of thousands of soldiers were strewn over the neighboring hills. King Sennacherib withdrew the remaining troops and returned to Nineveh.

I went to the temple and joined King Hezekiah and the others as we lifted our hands in praise to the Lord and sang,

> *I will extol the Lord at all times;*
> *his praise will always be on my lips...*
> *I sought the Lord and he answered me;*
> *and delivered me from all my fears...*
> *The angel of the Lord encamps around those who fear him;*
> *he saved him out of all his troubles.*
> (Ps 34:1,4,7)

14

THE DISCOVERY THAT LED TO REFORM

2 Kings 22 and 23

My name is Hilkiah, and I am from the tribe of Levi so was destined to become a priest in the service of the Lord. I began my apprenticeship in the temple when I was twenty while Manasseh was king of Judah. Many of priests of the Lord had relinquished their duties or forgotten how to perform them during his fifty-one year reign because the king had completely rejected the religious reforms of his father King Hezekiah and had forsaken the ways of the living God. All over the country, he erected altars to the sex god Baal. He practiced black magic, held séances, promoted the occult, and went so far as to sacrifice his own son as a burnt offering to Molek on the altar of Topheth in the valley of Ben Hinnom. Pagan worship was so widespread that many people no longer attended the religious services in the temple and quit coming to the yearly festivals. He filled the temple with idols to Baal and even erected two altars to the gods of the stars and placed them in both courtyards of the temple. It is true that towards the end of his reign, King Manasseh did repent, but he was unable to undo the pagan practices he had earlier promoted.

During this time, those of us who faithfully strove to serve the Lord found it most difficult to carry out the ceremonies and ritual duties at the temple. Let me give you an example of how frustrating and painful it was. Frequently, when we would prepare the morning or evening sacrifice, the pagan priests would dance around the altar making fun of us. Even after I was consecrated high priest during the two year reign of Ammon, Manasseh's son, who was no better than his father, I faced a brick wall when I tried to clean up the temple.

This was a very sad time for those of us who were faithful to the Lord our God. I recall on numerous occasions crying out to the Lord with words of the Psalmist,

> *For I endure scorn for your sake,*
> *and shame covers my face…*
> *for zeal for your house consumes me,*
> *and the insults of those who insult you fall on me.*
> (Ps 69: 7, 9)

Then I would remember these words and take heart,

> *Why, my soul, are you downcast?*
> *Why so disturbed within me?*
> *Put your hope in God,*
> *for I will yet praise him,*
> *my Savior and my God.*
> (Ps 42:5)

Things began to change after the young eight year old boy Josiah became king, thanks to the godly influence of his mother, Jedidah, who acted as regent until he came of age. At the age of sixteen, he started actively promoting the worship of the God of Israel and began to collect money in Jerusalem and Judah and even in some of the eastern districts for extensive repairs to the temple, which was in desperate need of them. He appointed supervisors to purchase timber and dressed stone and to oversee the work of the carpenters and stone masons.

One morning a few years back, one of the supervisors came to me and said, "Look what the workers found in one of the chambers under a pile of rubble."

He handed me a scroll that was covered with the accumulated dirt and dust of years. I put it on a table, carefully began to unroll it, and was able to make out the first line which read, *"These are the words Moses spoke to all Israel in the wilderness east of the Jordan,"* and a little further down I read, *"Moses proclaimed to the Israelites all that the Lord had commanded him concerning them."* (Dt 1:1,3)

It suddenly dawned on me that this was the book of the law that God had given to Moses. I couldn't believe my eyes. Years before when I started my service in the temple, some of the older priests had told me of the book of the law, but I had never seen it. That afternoon when Shaphan, the court secretary, came to see how the work of restoration was going, I showed him the scroll and told him it was the Book of God's Law. He took it and read it to the king, who became so troubled he tore his robes in anguish.

The next day Shaphan and various officials returned with this message from King Josiah, "The Lord must be furious with me and everyone else in Judah, because we and our ancestors have not obeyed the laws written in this book. Go find out what the Lord wants us to do."

We hurried off to consult Huldah, a prophetess, who lives in the northern part of the city. She is the wife of Shallum, who is keeper of the palace wardrobe. She said to us: "Go tell King Josiah that this is the message from the Lord: 'I am the Lord! I will destroy this country and everyone living here just as this book says. The people of Judah have turned against me. They have sacrificed to pagan gods and worshiped their idols. I am fed up with them. But I noticed how sad you were when you heard what this book says, and I heard your cry. So I will let you die in peace before the destruction comes.'"

After we reported to King Josiah what the Lord had said through the prophetess Huldah, he called for an assembly of all the people. A few weeks later when the delegates from the various districts, the civic and religious leaders, and the people had gathered in the temple courts, he read to them from the Book of God's Law. After he finished reading the scroll, he stood by the column reserved for the king, promised to obey the Lord and to follow the commands and the decrees that were written in the book. Then he asked the people to make the same promise. They all solemnly agreed to do this, thus renewing the covenant that God had made with his people.

He instructed me to order the priests and doorkeepers to go into the temple, gather all the articles used in the worship of Baal and the other pagan gods, burn them in the Kidron Valley, and scatter the ashes in the public cemetery. We tore down, smashed to pieces, and burned the altars King Manasseh had erected in the two courtyards of the temple. How happy I was to get rid of all these idolatrous pagan things!

The king ordered us to tear down the buildings next to the temple where the male prostitutes lived. He ordered men to desecrate the altar to Molech in the Hinnom Valley, just outside the city, where people sacrificed their children. He also destroyed the horses and chariots that were kept near the temple that some of the previous kings of Judah had used in their ceremonies to worship the sun god. He even closed the shrines that King Solomon had built to the disgusting gods and goddesses of Sidon, Moab, and Ammon and destroyed the stone images to these foreign gods.

The king even went to Bethel and destroyed the shrine, the altar, and the golden calf that Jeroboam, the first king of the northern kingdom of Israel, had made that caused his people to sin. He also destroyed all the pagan shrines in the north.

Then the king commanded that we celebrate the Passover. I prepared the temple, instructed the priests in their various duties, the king and his officials donated the animals for the sacrifices, and when everything was ready on the fourteenth day of the first month, we celebrated the Passover. The festivities went on for seven days. In the history of our people, we had never celebrated a Passover like this one, not even in the time of King Hezekiah.

The musicians played and I was so happy I began to sing:

> *How lovely is your dwelling place,*
> *O Lord of hosts!*
> *My soul longs, indeed it faints*

for the courts of the Lord;
my heart and my flesh
sing for joy to the living God.

Even the sparrow finds a home,
and the swallow a nest for herself,
where she may lay her young,
at your altars, O Lord of hosts,
my king and my God.
Happy are those who live in your house,
ever singing your praise.
For a day in your courts is better,
than a thousand elsewhere.
I would rather be a doorkeeper in
the house of my God
than live in the tents of wickedness.
O Lord of hosts,
happy is everyone who trusts in you.
(Ps 84:1-4, 10, 12)

15

THE KING WHO
BURNED A SCROLL

Jeremiah 7, 26, 36, 45

My name is Baruch, and I have been the prophet Jeremiah's scribe for many years. Because his prophetic ministry has been so important, I would like to share with you excerpts from some of his messages and incidents from his life during the critical reigns of Kings Jehoiakim and Zedekiah of Judah.

Jeremiah started his prophetic ministry during the reign of King Josiah. He soon realized that though the king was faithful to the Lord and tried his best to bring religious and moral renewal to Judah, the pagan influences of the previous king, Manasseh, were so profound and widespread that Josiah's reforms did not have much lasting effect. Jeremiah believed that even though Josiah had reestablished the covenant with the Lord, the people had broken it by their idolatrous and evil practices.

When Josiah learned that Pharaoh Necho of Egypt was leading his troops north to support the crumbling Assyrian empire, he tried to stop him at the pass of Megiddo, and he was killed in the ensuing battle. When Necho returned from this campaign, he captured our new king,

Jehoahaz, at Riblah and carried him off to Egypt in chains. He put Eliakim, Jehoahaz's older brother, on the throne of Judah, changed his name to Jehoiakim, and imposed on him a heavy tribute.

Some years later, Necho went north again, but this time he was defeated by the Babylonian army at the battle of Carchemish. I was relieved when I heard this news, for he who had troubled us for so long would trouble us no longer. But I also feared that the victor, the king of Babylon, would send his army south to extend his power and make sure no country rebelled against his authority.

Sometime later, in a lengthy sermon at the gate of the courtyard of the temple, Jeremiah warned the people that if they did not repent, God would destroy the city of Jerusalem and the temple. The leaders and the people responded by affirming that since God was in his temple, he would surely protect it and, by extension, protect them. This was Jeremiah's stinging reply, *"Hear the word of the Lord…Will you steal and murder, commit adultery and perjury, burn incense to Baal and follow other gods you have not known, and then come and stand before me in this house, which bears my Name, and say, 'We are safe' ___safe to do all these detestable things? Has this house, which bears my Name, become a den of robbers?"* (Jer 7:1,9-10) He answered his own question by warning the people not to believe in false predictions of peace, and he repeated the message from God,

> *"I will make Jerusalem a heap of ruins, a haunt of jackals;*
> *and I will lay waste to the towns of Judah,*
> *so no one can live there.*
> (Jer 9:11)

About a year after we heard the news of the victory of the king of Babylon at the battle of Carchemish, Jeremiah again addressed the people. He reminded them that since the thirteenth year of the reign of King Josiah to the present, a total of twenty- three years, he had repeatedly been exhorting them to repent of their evil ways and return to the Lord, but, since they had persistently refused to obey, the Lord God had given him this word:

*"Because you have not listened to my words, I will summon all the
people of the north and my servant Nebuchadnezzar, king of Babylon,
and I will bring them against this land and its inhabitants and against
all the surrounding nations. I will completely destroy them and make
them an object of horror and scorn, and an everlasting ruin. I will
banish from them the sounds of joy and gladness, the voices of bride
and bridegroom, the sound of millstones and the light of the lamp.*
(Jer 25:8-10)

About this time, on instructions from the Lord, Jeremiah decided
to write down all the messages God had given him from the time of
Josiah until the present. After he summoned me, he began dictating to
me all the words from the Lord, and I wrote them down on a scroll. The
process was long and wearisome, and the messages were so threatening
and depressing, that I said to the prophet, "These messages of doom
keep piling up, one after another. This is scary, for, if all this predicted
destruction takes place, what will happen to us?"

Jeremiah replied, "Things are going to get worse before they get
better, but don't worry, God will take care of us through this whole
situation."

A few months later, we learned that the king of Babylon, after
marching south along the coast, had attacked, captured, and sacked the
Philistine city of Ashkelon. King Jehoiakim was so alarmed he decided to
gather the residents of Jerusalem and the neighboring towns and villages
in the temple courts to celebrate a fast. He would request the protection
of the God of Israel and of the other gods that were being worshiped
throughout the land.

Jeremiah decided to take advantage of this event. He had been
prohibited from preaching in the temple because of his threatening
sermons, so he instructed me to go and read from the scroll to all the
people gathered there.

I climbed the steps to the upper courtyard at the entrance to the
New Gate of the temple. From the balcony of the room of Gemariah,
the temple secretary, I read the words of the scroll to the people. When
Gemariah's son, Micaiah, heard the words of the scroll, he went to the

royal palace and told the king's officials, who were sitting in the secretary's room, what he had heard. They immediately instructed Jehudi to go find me and have me bring the scroll. When I arrived, they asked me to please read the scroll. As I read, they were overcome with fear, and, after conferring among themselves, came to the conclusion that they must report this to the king.

They asked me, *"Tell us, how did you come to write all this? Did Jeremiah dictate it?*

I answered, *"Yes, he dictated all these words to me, and I wrote them in ink on the scroll."* (Jer 36:17,18)

Then they said, "You and Jeremiah must go and hide right away."

I took their advice and rushed over to Jeremiah's house to tell him we had better find a safe place because I knew the king would be after us.

Later, one of the king's assistants told me what happened. He said the officials hid the scroll in the palace secretary's room and then went to the king, who was sitting in the courtyard of the winter apartment, warming himself. There was a fire in a brazier because it was bitter cold. When the officials reported what they had heard, the king sent Jehudi to get the scroll.

After Jehudi returned, all the officials gathered around King Jehoiakim, and Jehudi began unwinding the scroll and slowly reading it, so everyone could hear. Whenever he finished reading two or three columns, the king would cut them off with a scribe's knife and toss them into the fire. Even though three of his officials, Elnathan, Delaiah and Gemariah urged the king not to burn the scroll, he refused to listen to them. The king and most of his other assistants showed no fear, nor remorse. Instead, when Jehudi had finished reading the scroll, and the king had burned it all, he turned and said to two of his assistants in an angry tone: "Enough of that doom and destruction, now that we have finished with that, be gone and arrest those two troublemakers, Jeremiah and Baruch."

While we were hiding, Jeremiah procured another scroll and dictated to me all the messages of the first scroll and added many others. And there was an additional word from the Lord, *Therefore this is what the Lord says about Jehoiakim king of Judah: I will punish him and his children* and his attendants for their wickedness; I will bring on them and those living in Jerusalem and the people of Judah every disaster I pronounced against them, because they have not listened. (Jer 36:30, 31)

The total disregard of the king, the priests, the elders, and the people for the messages from the Lord deeply troubled Jeremiah. One morning I heard him pour out his complaint to God:

> You deceived me, Lord, and I was deceived;
> you overpowered me and prevailed.
> I am ridiculed all day long;
> everyone mocks me.
> Whenever I speak out, I cry out
> proclaiming violence and destruction.
> So the word of the Lord has brought me
> insult and reproach all day long.
> But if I say, "I will not mention his word
> or speak anymore in his name,
> his word is in my heart like a fire,
> a fire shut up in my bones.
> I am weary of holding it in;
> indeed I cannot.
> (Jer 20:7-9)

I also observed how painful it was for him to have to preach the message of doom which the Lord had given him. One day he said to me:

> Since my people are crushed, I am crushed;
> I mourn, and horror grips me.
> Is there no balm in Gilead?
> Oh, that my head were a spring of water
> and my eyes a fountain of tears!
> I would weep day and night
> for the slain of my people.
> (Jer 8:21-9:1)

But Jeremiah was convinced that even though he had been entrusted him with messages of doom, destruction, and exile, the Lord would ultimately bring his people back and pour out his blessing on them:

He said to me: *"The days are coming," declares the Lord, "when it will no longer be said, 'As surely as the Lord lives, who brought the Israelites up out of Egypt,' but it will be said, 'As surely as the Lord lives, who brought the Israelites up out of the land of the north and out of all the countries where he had banished them.' For I will restore them to the land I gave their ancestors."* (Jer 16:14,15)

But even more important, he believed God would make a new covenant with his people. On another occasion he relayed this message from the Lord:

> *"This is the covenant I will make with the people of Israel...*
> *I will put my law in their minds and write it on their hearts.*
> *I will be their God, and they will be my people.*
> *No longer will they teach their neighbor,*
> *or say to one another, 'Know the Lord,'*
> *because they will all know me,*
> *from the least of them to the greatest.*
> *For I will forgive their wickedness*
> *and will remember their sins no more."*
> (Jer 31:33 34)

16

JEREMIAH AND THE FALL OF JERUSALEM

Jeremiah 21, 22, 28, 32, 34, 38, 39

Now let me, Baruch, tell you about Jeremiah's prophetic ministry during the reign of King Zedekiah and share with you some of the incidents that led to the tragic end of it all. But again, I must give a little background information, so you can understand better what happened and why it happened.

Shortly after the burning of the scroll, Nebuchadnezzar did invade Judah. King Jehoiakim had to surrender and was required to pay a yearly tribute. Three years later, Jehoiakim rebelled and refused to pay the tribute money any longer. Nebuchadnezzar's response was firm and decisive, but before his army arrived at the gates of Jerusalem, Jehoiakim died, and Jehoiachin, his son, had to deal with the consequences of his father's rebellion The Babylonian army surrounded the city, and the young king had no option but to surrender.

Nebuchadnezzar took the king and his mother, the palace attendants and officials, many of the leading citizens of the city, and most of the skilled workers and artisans, a total of ten thousand inhabitants, and seven thousand officers and soldiers, and deported them to Babylon. He left only the poorest people of the city. He also raided the temple and took the silver and gold articles made during the time of Solomon. Then he made Mattaniah, another of Josiah's sons, king and changed his name to Zedekiah.

Early in the reign of Zedekiah, Jeremiah attacked the injustice he saw at the highest levels of government. He went to the king's palace and proclaimed this message, "*This is what the Lord says, 'Do what is just and right. Rescue from the hand of the oppressor the one who has been robbed. Do no wrong or violence to the foreigner, the fatherless, the widow, and do not shed innocent blood in this place.'*"

And then he added,

> "*Woe to him who builds his palace by unrighteousness,*
> *his upper rooms by injustice,*
> *making his own people work for nothing,*
> *not paying them for their labor.*"
> (Jer 22:3, 13)

Of course, this message did not sit well with the king and his officials. There were prophets running around proclaiming a message of false hope. One of them Hananiah confronted Jeremiah in the Temple in front of the priests and all the people and said, "This is the message I have from the Lord, the Almighty God of Israel. I will break the yoke of the king of Babylon. Before two years are up, I'll bring back all the silver and gold articles from the temple that Nebuchadnezzar took to Babylon, and, not only that, I'll see that the exiled king and all the people in Babylon get back home."

Jeremiah responded with these words, "That's wonderful! I wish what you're preaching were true -- that God would bring back the articles from the temple and all of the exiles who were taken to Babylon. Listen to me, many of the prophets before me preached war, disaster, and destruction upon many countries and kingdoms, but the prophet who preaches peace will be recognized as one sent by God only if peace arrives."

Jeremiah was wearing a yoke of straps and crossbars on his neck as a symbol of the oppression that was coming. Hananiah went up to

Jeremiah, yanked off the yoke, broke it, and said, "The Lord says, 'in the same way, in two years, I will break the yoke of Nebuchadnezzar off the neck of all the nations.'"

As we were walking away, I asked Jeremiah, "How can you be so sure Hananiah is not right?"

Jeremiah replied, "Just wait and see who's right."

Reports began to come in about the Babylonian army's advance and the attacks on the cities of Lachish and Azekah only forty miles away. Then one morning, we awoke to find Jerusalem surrounded by the Babylonian army. Immediately King Zedekiah sent two prominent citizens to ask Jeremiah if there was a word from the Lord, reminding the prophet that when the Assyrian army besieged the city in the reign of King Hezekiah, the Lord had miraculously delivered us.

I was distressed when the prophet said to them: "Yes, I do have a message from the Lord. He says, 'I have decided to side in with the Babylonians and support them. In my fierce anger, I am ready to wipe out the inhabitants of Judah, including you, and will deliver you and your corrupt officials into the hands of the King of Babylon.'"

But he also made the options quite clear: "And tell all the people to listen very carefully to the message I have from the Lord for them, 'I am showing you two paths, one leads to death, the other to life. All of those who stay in the city will die by the sword, hunger, or disease. All of those who go out and surrender to the Babylonians, who are besieging the city, will live. Choose the best path, for I am going to destroy this city.'"

The commander of the Babylonian army received word that an Egyptian army was moving north to attack him, so he lifted the siege briefly while he deployed some his forces to repel the attack. Zedekiah took this as a sign of God's intervention, and, in an attempt to correct some of the injustice, he decreed freedom for all the slaves in the city. But no sooner had they been freed, than the officials and others changed their minds and enslaved them again.

Jeremiah responded angrily to this and said, "You decreed freedom for all your slaves, which was pleasing to the Lord, but then changed your mind, so the Lord says, 'I proclaim freedom for all of you, freedom to die by the sword, hunger, and plague.'"

When the Babylonian general returned, the siege was tightened, the battering rams and other siege ramps were put in place, and the assault began. The defenders of the city took bricks and stones from many of the buildings in an attempt to bolster up the defenses. There was nothing more to do but wait for the end. Food supplies were running low. It was all I could do to find some bread for Jeremiah, who was held in the courtyard. Famine was spreading. It was an awful sight to see the gaunt figures of those stumbling along the streets looking for food. What shook me to the core was when a woman who lived down the street from Jeremiah's house, cooked her own child to feed its siblings. (La 4:10)

Jeremiah's message that whoever would go over to the Babylonians would live while those who remained in the city would perish, upset the king's officials. They went to King Zedekiah and reported that the prophet was undermining the loyalty of the soldiers and promoting the ruin of the nation. The king handed Jeremiah over to them, and they lowered him into a cistern that was in the courtyard where he was being held, and he sank in the mud.

Ebed-Melek, an Ethiopian, who was a secret sympathizer of Jeremiah and also an official in the palace, heard what had happened. He went to Zechariah to tell him that the prophet would probably die in the cistern. The king granted him permission to rescue the prophet, so he went to a room under the treasury, found some old rags and clothes, and let them down into the cistern with some ropes. He instructed Jeremiah to put the rags under his arm pits, and Ebed-Melek and the men with him lifted him out.

Jeremiah told me that King Zedekiah sought him out once more, and in private said to him, "I am going to ask you a question. Don't hide the answer from me."

"If I give you an answer, will you kill me?" asked Jeremiah. "If I give you advice you won't listen to me."

The king said, "I solemnly promise you that as the Lord lives I will not kill you, nor hand you over to those who want to do so."

Jeremiah said, "Quit dilly-dallying!" and then repeated the message from the Lord, "If you surrender to the generals of the king of Babylon, your life will be spared, and the city will not be burned down. But if you do not surrender, they will burn the city, and you will not escape."

Zedekiah said, "But I'm afraid of the Jews who have already deserted to the Baylonians. The Babylonians will turn me over to the Jews who will torture me."

"They will not hand you over to the Jews," replied Jeremiah. "Obey the Lord, and do what I am telling you. It will be to your benefit, and you will live.

After a further brief interchange of words, Zechariah said to him, "Don't let any one know about our conversation. If my officials ask you what we talked about, tell them that you were pleading with me not to put you back in the cistern."

Jeremiah did what the king had asked him to do, and no one knew of their conversation.

On the afternoon of the ninth day, of the fourth month, of the eleventh year of King Zechariah's reign, after a siege of eighteen months, the Babylonians made a breach in the wall of the city, and the enemy troops poured in. The generals and principal officers set themselves up as a ruling council near the middle gate of the city. When Zedekiah, his family, his court officials, and the soldiers saw this, they fled that very night, leaving the city by the way of the garden gate and went into the wilderness.

The Babylonian army pursued them and overtook them at Jericho. They captured Zechariah and took him to Riblah where King Nebuchadnezzar determined his fate. The soldiers killed Zechariah's sons in front of him, then proceeded to kill the court officials, and finally blinded the king and deported him to Babylon.

One month later, Nebuzaradan, the commander of the Babylonian imperial guard, came and broke down the city walls, set fire to the temple, the royal palace, and all the important buildings and principal houses. He completely destroyed the city and carried into exile most of the remaining inhabitants and all of the remaining articles of the Temple.

Later, when Nebuzaradan found Jeremiah, who was in chains, and me, among the captives that were being carried into exile, he released him and invited him to go to Babylon with him as a freed man, but Jeremiah chose to remain in Jerusalem. The commander gave him provisions and let us go.

Finally, I must tell you about a simple, though extraordinary, incident, that occurred shortly before the fall of the city, while Jeremiah was confined to the courtyard of the guard. Hanamel, Jeremiah's cousin, came to him and offered to sell him his field in Jeremiah's hometown of Anathoth because, by law, Jeremiah had the first right of refusal. Jeremiah bought it, gave his cousin the money, signed the deed in the presence of witnesses, and sealed it. He gave it to me with instructions to put the original deed and a copy in a clay jar, for them to be kept for a long time.

He said, with hope ringing in his voice, "I believe that houses, fields and vineyards will again be bought in this land. Write these words in a book: *This is what the Lord, the God of Israel says, 'The days are coming when I will bring my people Israel and Judah back from captivity and restore them to the land I gave their ancestors to possess.* (Jer 30:2, 3) *They will be my people, and I will be their God. I will give them singleness of heart and action, so that they will always fear me and that all will then go well for them and their children after them … I will rejoice in doing them good and will assuredly plant them in this land with all my heart and soul'"* (Jer 32:38-41)

17

ZERUBABEL REBUILDS THE TEMPLE

Ezra and selected passages from Zechariah

Shortly after Cyrus, King of the Persians, conquered the city of Babylon, the Lord God moved the heart of the king to make this amazing proclamation:

"The Lord, the God of heaven…, has appointed me to build a temple for him at Jerusalem. Any of his people among you may go up to Jerusalem in Judah and build the temple of the Lord, the God of Israel, the God who is in Jerusalem, and may their God be with them." (Ezra 1:2, 3)

I received this proclamation with great joy, and since I am the direct heir to the throne of David, grandson of exiled King Jehoiachin, Cyrus appointed me, Zerubbabel, to be his representative. In my civic duties I use the name Sheshbazzar, which the Babylonians have given me.

King Cyrus gave the order for the 5,400 articles of gold and silver belonging to the temple, which Nebuchadnezzar had carried away, to be entrusted to me to take back to Jerusalem. After making careful preparations and spreading the word, I was able to gather 42,000 of the exiled Jews and lead them back to our land. Joshua, the chief priest who accompanied me, and I were most happy to fulfill the wish of King Cyrus to rebuild the temple of God.

Shortly after we arrived in Jerusalem, the first order of business was to erect an altar on which to offer our sacrifices of thanksgiving to the Lord. We requested the people of Tyre and Sidon to cut cedar logs from the forests of Lebanon and ship them by sea to Joppa. The Levites were appointed to supervise the construction. We paid masons and carpenters to prepare the stone and wood, and, two years after our arrival, we began to rebuild the temple.

When the foundations were laid, we celebrated the Festival of Tabernacles. We sang this chorus to the Lord with trumpets and cymbals.

He is good; his love toward Israel endures forever. (Ezr 3:11)

Almost all the people gave a shout of joy, but a few older folk, who had seen the Temple of Solomon, wept when they saw the more modest dimensions of the present foundations.

I should have known that there would be opposition to the project, but I did not expect it to start the way it did. When people of the neighboring regions got wind of what we were doing, they came and offered to help us. They said they liked us and had been worshipping the same God. Joshua and I conferred with the elders and leaders of the people, and we perceived that this was some kind of trick. I told these delegates that we alone would build our temple. They withdrew, but some time later, we learned of their campaign to discourage and even threaten our people and bribe some of our leaders. The opposition became so severe that I considered it prudent to suspend the work.

In the meantime, we had begun to build our houses, and when the prophet Haggai arrived, his words pricked our consciences. He preached, *"Is it a time for you yourselves to be living in your paneled houses, while this house remains a ruin?... You have planted much, but harvested little. You eat, but never have enough. You drink, but never have your fill. You put on clothes, but are not warm. You earn wages, only to put them in a purse with holes in it... Why? Because of my house, which remains a ruin, while each of you is busy with his own house... The time has come to rebuild the house of the Lord.* (Hag 1:2, 4, 5, 6, 9)

Later, when the prophet Zechariah arrived, he had a message specifically for me, *"This is the word of the Lord to Zerubbabel: 'Not by might nor by power, but my Spirit', says the Lord Almighty… The hands of Zerubbabel have laid the foundation of this temple; his hands will also complete it. Let your hands be strong so that the temple may be built.'* (Zec 4:6, 8; 8:9)

These words and the words of Haggai were a powerful incentive to start the project again. I decided to obey the Lord even in the face of opposition and rallied the people to do the same. Eighteen years after the work had been suspended, we took up the construction again.

No sooner had we begun to rebuild the temple than Tattenai, the provincial governor of the region of Trans-Euphrates, and his assistants came and asked me who had authorized the renewing of the work and requested the names of those involved in the construction. I was afraid this meant they were going to file another report against us. I explained to them that the Lord God wanted the temple rebuilt, the temple that had been built by King Solomon many years before and destroyed by the king of Babylon. King Cyrus had issued a decree authorizing me to supervise the construction.

Later, Tattenai told me he wrote a letter to the new king, Darius, explaining this whole matter and asking him to search in the royal archives of Babylon to see if King Cyrus had in fact issued such a decree.

A few months went by, and when Tattenai returned, he showed me the letter in which King Darius had responded to his inquiry. The king wrote that his assistants carried out the search and found a scroll on which there was a memorandum from King Cyrus authorizing the rebuilding of the temple. I quote from the letter: "Tattenai, you and your officials, *stay away from there. Do not interfere with the work on this temple of God. Let the governor of the Jews and the Jewish elders rebuild this house of God on its site.* (Ezr 6:6, 7)

Then Darius goes on to instruct Tattenai and his assistants to aid us by providing funds from the royal treasury and whatever else is needed. This was truly an answer to our prayers. Praise the Lord our God!

On the third day of the twelfth month, in the sixth year of the reign of Darius, we finished rebuilding the temple. We installed the priests and

Levites, made the appropriate sacrifices, and celebrated the dedication with great joy and songs of thanksgiving to God for his faithfulness. I asked the prophet Zechariah to preach the sermon for the dedication, and he challenged us with these words:

"This is what the Lord Almighty says, 'I have determined to do good again to Jerusalem and Judah. Do not be afraid. These are the things you are to do: Speak the truth to each other, and render true and sound judgment in your courts, do not plot evil against each other, and do not love to swear falsely." (Zec 8:15-17)

I remember especially these words: *"Once again men and women of ripe old age will sit in the streets of Jerusalem, each of them with a cane in hand because of their age. The city streets will be filled with boys and girls playing there... The Lord their God will save his people on that day as a shepherd saves his flock. They will sparkle in his land like jewels in a crown."* (Zec 8:4,5; 9:16)

When I looked around and saw so much of the city still in ruins, his words were particularly comforting. He concluded his message with this amazing promise: *"This is what the Lord says: 'I will return to Zion and dwell in Jerusalem. Then Jerusalem will be called the Faithful City, and the mountain of the Lord Almighty will be called the Holy Mountain."* (Zec 8:3)

18

A BEAUTY QUEEN SAVES HER PEOPLE

The book of Esther

My name is Mordecai. I am from the tribe of Benjamin, and I live in Susa, the capital of the Persian Empire. My parents were exiled along with King Jehoiachin in the first deportation of the Jews under Nebuchadnezzar. The exile has not been all that bad, and many of us have put down roots and prospered in this land.

Let me tell you about something important that happened here under the present king, Xerxes, the immediate successor of King Darius. The king held a big fancy banquet in his elegant palace for the nobles from many of the 127 provinces of the empire. After the king had enjoyed too much wine, he ordered Queen Vashti to come and show off her beauty, but she refused because of the indignity. The king was angry and his advisors were worried that this incident might become an example for the women of the empire to disobey their husbands, so she was stripped of her royal position and placed in permanent seclusion.

The king's advisors suggested that a beauty pageant be held in the capital for the king to choose his future queen from among the most beautiful women of the empire. I submitted the name of my cousin

Hadasah, whom I had brought up and adopted, because she was an orphan. I thought she was extraordinarily beautiful. She was chosen as a candidate, and after months of preparation, during which the girls were fed a special diet and given beauty treatments, the contest was held in the palace. My cousin, whom I call Esther, won the favor of the king. He celebrated a big banquet and crowned her his queen. What an honor for all of us Jews to have one of our own as queen. Nevertheless, I advised Esther it would not be prudent to reveal her ethnic identity.

One day when I was sitting by the doorway to the palace waiting to be admitted to visit Queen Esther, I accidentally learned that two of the officers who guarded the palace had become disgruntled over something and were planning to assassinate the king. While I was visiting my cousin, I told her of the plot. Later she informed the king who found the plot to be true and had the two men executed.

About this time King Xerxes selected a man by the name Haman and exalted him to one of the highest positions in the kingdom. This bothered me because I knew Haman had been involved in some shady deals, so whenever I ran across him I refused to give him the customary signs of respect. I could tell it irked Haman. Some of the king's officials, whom I had befriended and who knew I was a Jew, chided me about this.

One of the king's officials who is my close friend came to my house and told me that Haman had proposed to the king the extermination of all the Jews in the empire. Haman's argument was that we keep ourselves separate and our customs are different from those of other people. He feels that it is not in the best interest of the kingdom to tolerate us. He was willing to deposit multiple pounds of silver in the royal treasury for the expense of carrying out the project. The king has approved the proposal and has given Haman his own signet ring.

The official also told me that the secretaries were called to the palace to write out the edict in the script and language of the people of each province, and Haman signed the copies with the king's signet ring. Couriers have been sent out to all the provinces with the order to kill all the Jews and plunder their goods on the thirteenth day of the twelfth month. And then he gave me a copy of the edict.

I fell prostrate on the floor and pled with the Lord to give me courage and wisdom. Then I tore my clothes, put on sackcloth, threw ashes on my head, and went out into the main square of the city and up to the gate of the palace weeping bitterly. Some of the attendants saw me and told the queen who immediately sent Hathak, one of the king's trusted eunuchs assigned to her service, with fresh clothes for me and to ask what was troubling me. Apparently, she was ignorant of the royal edict.

I gave him a copy of the text of the edict, told him to show it to the queen, explain the whole matter to her, and instruct her to go to the king and plead for mercy for all the Jews.

The queen received the news and immediately told Hathak to report back to me that the law of the Medes and Persians, which cannot be broken, states that anyone who enters the presence of the king in the inner court without being summoned faces death, unless the king extends his royal scepter to that person. She also said that it has been a month since the king requested her presence.

I said to Hathak: "Tell the queen, don't for a moment think that because you're the queen and live in the king's palace you are the one Jew who is going to be spared. If you remain silent at this time, I am sure God will send us help from somewhere else, but you and our whole family will be eliminated. *Who knows? Maybe you were made queen for such a time as this.*" (Est 4:14 *The Message*)

Esther replied, instructing me to gather all the Jews in Susa, get them to fast for three days, and she would do the same with her attendants. She said, "At the end of the three days, even though it is against the law, I'll go into the king's throne room, and if I die, I die."

I did as she instructed me. Then I went home and fasted for three days. The evening of the third day I could not sleep, so I spent the night in prayer. I remembered the words of the Psalmist and held them up before God:

> *Do not hold against us the sins of past generations;*
> *may your mercy come quickly to meet us,*
> *for we are in desperate need.*
> *Help us, God our Savior,*

for the glory of your name;
deliver us and forgive our sins
for your name's sake.
Ps 79:8,9

On the morning of the fourth day, I heard a knock on the front door. When I opened it, there was Hathak with a big smile on his face. He reported: "Yesterday afternoon, Esther dressed in her finest and looking very sexy went to the door of the throne room. When the king saw her he smiled, beckoned her to come in, extended his golden scepter towards her and asked what was her request. She invited him and Haman to dinner that evening, and during dinner the king asked her again what she wanted. She said she wanted to invite them to a special banquet she would prepare the next day when she would present her request to the king.

No sooner had Hathak left, than a messenger arrived from the king requesting my immediate presence at the courtyard of the palace. I rushed over there and found Haman, looking like a storm, holding the reins of one of the king's horses. He draped one of the royal robes over my shoulders, ordered me to get on the horse, and began leading me through the streets of the city proclaiming in a loud angry voice, "This is what the king does for the man he honors." This strange behavior left me completely befuddled. I could not for the life of me figure out what was going on.

When we got back to the courtyard, Haman dropped the reins of the horse, and took off running down the street. Hathak was waiting for me. I jumped down from the horse and asked him: "What on earth is going on?"

He replied, "A strange thing happened last night. The king could not sleep, so he asked me to get the book in which the events of the reign are recorded and read It to him. I happened to find the report of how you exposed the plot of the two guards to murder the king. He stopped me and asked if anything had been done to honor you, and I replied that I didn't think so. In the morning he sent a messenger to get you. When Haman arrived, the king ordered him to lead you around the city on one of the palace horses dressed in one of the royal robes, as a way to honor you for what you had done."

"No wonder he ran off, humiliated and upset," I replied

That night it wasn't the king who couldn't sleep. It was me. I tossed and turned all night wondering what might be the outcome of the banquet to which Esther had invited the king and Haman. The next morning, since I couldn't wait for Hathak to bring me the news, I rushed off to the palace and waited anxiously for him in the courtyard. I saw him running down the steps, and when he reached me, he threw his arms around me in a big hug and then burst out: "You and your people are saved. Last night at the banquet, as the king and Haman were drinking their wine, the king asked the queen to reveal her request. She said, 'I beg your Majesty, if it pleases you grant me and my people life. If we were to be sold into slavery I would not have bothered you, but we have been sold to be massacred and exterminated.' The king asked Queen Esther who had dared to plan such a murderous thing and where he was. She then said, 'A vile enemy,' and pointing to Haman added, 'This man, Haman.'"

"The king flew into a rage, and went out into the courtyard to try to control himself. Haman was terrified, threw himself on the couch where the queen was reclining, and begged for mercy.

"Just then the king returned and when he saw Haman groveling by the couch, he cried out, 'Will he even molest the queen in the brief moment when I stepped out?'

"And the king had Haman hung on the gallows he had prepared for you."

I burst out singing and dancing for joy:

> *It is good to praise the Lord*
> *and make music to your name, O Most High…*
> *For you make me glad by your deed, Lord;*
> *I sing for joy at what your hands have done.*
> *My eyes have seen the defeat of my adversaries;*
> *my ears have heard the rout of my wicked foes.*
> (Ps 92:1, 4, 11)

When the king learned that the queen was my cousin, he took the signet ring he had retrieved from Haman and gave it to me. The king authorized me to write out a new edict, protecting the lives of all the Jews. I signed it with the king's signet, the edict was translated into all the languages of the empire, and copies were sent out to all the provinces.

I invited all the Jews from this time forth to celebrate a special feast each year to commemorate their deliverance from their enemies. I suggested that the festival be celebrated on the same dates as the proposed pogrom, the fourteenth and fifteenth days of the twelfth month, the month of Adar. Since these dates had been chosen by lot, called in the Persian language *pur*, I suggested that this feast be called the *Feast of Purim*.

19

NEHEMIAH REBUILDS
THE WALLS

The book of Nehemiah

I was overjoyed to see my brother, Hanani, and some companions who had just arrived from Judah. After we shared a bear hug, I asked him: "How are things going in Judah?"

He sighed deeply and replied, "Not too good. The people are in trouble, and the walls of the city are rubble."

This news made me very sad, and I decided to fast for a few days and dedicate myself to prayer. In my prayers I confessed our sin and reminded the Lord that if we obeyed his commands and were faithful to him, he had promised to return his people from their exile to their land. On the last day of my fast, I prayed, "O Lord God, I have decided to present my petition to the king. Please grant me favor in his presence and give me success."

I was living in the city of Susa, capital of the Persian Empire. It was the twentieth year of the reign of King Artaxerxes, the successor or Xerxes, and I had been his cup bearer and wine taster for some time. On a warm spring day in the month of Nisan, I served the king his cup of wine, and when he saw my face he said, "Nehemiah, why do you look so sad? If you're not sick, something must be troubling you."

I was trembling with fear when I addressed the king, "Great king, I am very sad because the city where my ancestors are buried is in ruins with its walls and gates destroyed."

"What do you want to do about it?" asked the king.

I prayed silently to God asking for wisdom and replied, "If it would please you, and if I your servant have found favor before you, send me to rebuild that city."

After we had set a date for my departure, I requested that the king provide me with letters to the provincial governors of the provinces of Trans-Euphrates and authorize the keeper of the royal forest to provide timber for the beams of the gates. He graciously granted my requests and appointed me governor of Judah.

After a journey of over seven hundred miles, I arrived in Jerusalem. Three nights later, under the light of a full moon, I got a horse, took some men with me, and we made an inspection tour of the walls of the city. The walls and the gates were in shambles. I did not share with the priests and the officials of the city my intentions until the next day, when I gathered them and said, "I have seen the condition of the walls and the gates of the city. Therefore, I invite you to join me in rebuilding them, and let me assure you that I have permission from King Artaxerxes for this project."

I made specific plans and set about gathering the timber and the stone we needed. I assigned the different sections of the wall and the corresponding gates to different families and groups of people.

When Sanballat, an influential citizen of Samaria, heard we were rebuilding the walls, he came and ridiculed our work. His words stung, "You weak-kneed Jews think you are going to finish this project in a day. Ha! You can't bring back to life stones that are buried in rubble."

And then his companion, Tobiah, piped up, *"Even a fox climbing up on it would break down this wall of stones."* (Ne 4:3)

After hearing their taunts and insults, I lifted up my heart in prayer to God, "O Lord, you see how we are despised by these men. You have heard their taunts. *Turn their insults back on their heads.*"

All the people worked hard. When Sanballat and his companions realized we had the walls half way up and the gaps were being closed, they hatched a plot to infiltrate our work force and kill those actively engaged in the rebuilding. Some neighbors who lived near these men told us about the plot. I positioned men, armed with swords and spears, at strategic places along the wall. After the threat from Sanballat was over, I deployed half of the men to work while half stood guard. Since our workforce was thinly spread out along the length of the wall, I assigned a trumpeter to sound an alarm in case of an imminent attack so as to gather all the men in one place. I assured the people that our great and awesome God would defend us and our families.

Shortly before we finished rebuilding the wall, Sanballat and Tobiah cooked up another scheme. They sent messengers to invite me to meet with them in a neighboring village. I feared that this might be a trap to capture and kill me, so I refused to meet them. I sent word that I was working on an important project and could not leave it. Four times they sent messengers. The fifth time, Sanballat sent his aide with a letter for me in which he said he had heard that we were going to revolt, and that the Jews were going to proclaim me king. He said that this report would get back to the king and reminded me that Artxerxes was already a king over Judah. He suggested that for my own health it would be better if we met. In my reply, I assured him that nothing like what he implied was taking place; it was all in his head.

Ezra is a priest and teacher of the law who led a group of one thousand seven hundred Jews back to Jerusalem thirteen years ago. He and I decided to order and reorganize the social and religious life of the people before dedicating the walls.

Since coming to Jerusalem, I had observed some injustices that I needed to address. Some of the leaders and more prosperous Jews were taking advantage of the poor people by making them mortgage their lands at exorbitant interest rates so they could buy grain. I realized that my brothers and I were also guilty of charging high interest rates on loans to the people, so we pledged to suspend any interest payments and exhorted the rich to do the same. The debts some people had incurred were so burdensome that they had to sell their children as slaves. In order to alleviate the burden, my brothers and I no longer took any of the grain allotted for the governor and his family and did not demand any payment for our services.

Ezra called for an assembly of all the people to instruct them in the Law of God. He had a wooden platform erected in the town square in front of the Water Gate and, for seven days, stood on it, and read from the Book of the Law of God from day break till noon. He read carefully and stopped frequently for the priests to explain to the people what was being read, so they could understand clearly the Law of God.

Ezra came to the section where the Lord orders the people to live in temporary shelters during a festival in the seventh month, to recall their sojourn through the wilderness before entering the promised land. Upon hearing this, the people scattered to gather branches and build rustic shelters to celebrate the Feast of Tabernacles. This festival had not been celebrated like this since the time of Joshua.

As Ezra read the Law of God, we realized how far we had strayed from the path of the Lord, and a sense of guilt came over us all. On the twenty-fourth day of the same month we held a great assembly of the elders, officials, priests, and all the people. After hearing a lengthy review of our history, we confessed our sins and the sins of our ancestors before God, asking him to forgive us. Then we made an agreement not to intermarry with our pagan neighbors, to observe the Sabbath, to bring the first-fruits of our crops to the Lord, and to observe the other ordinances set forth in the Book of the Law. The priests and leaders put the agreement in writing and sealed it.

Amazing as it may seem, we finished rebuilding the wall in fifty-two days. To celebrate the dedication of the wall, the priests first purified themselves ceremonially and then purified the people, the gates, and the wall. Then the leaders of the people took their places alongside the wall, and two enormous choirs with their musicians were assigned to give thanks. The first choir, with half of the people following, started its procession at the Dung Gate, at the extreme southern tip of the wall, went north on the east side of the city to the Fountain Gate, up the steps of the City of David, past the ruins of David's ancient palace and the

Water Gate, into the courtyard of the temple. Along the way they sang from one of the Psalms:

> *I rejoiced with those who said to me,*
> *'Let us go to the house of the Lord.'*
> *Our feet are standing in your gates, Jerusalem.*
> *Pray for the peace of Jerusalem:*
> *"May those who love you be secure".*
> *For the sake of my family and friends,*
> *I will say, "Peace be within you."*
> (Ps 122:1,2,6, 8)

The second choir, with me and the other half of the people following, started its procession on the west side of the city at the Tower of the Ovens, along the Broad Wall. We went up to the Old Gate, turned east to the Fish Gate, went on past the Tower of Hananel, and turned south through the Sheep Gate toward the courtyard of the temple, singing on the way from another Psalm:

> *For the Lord has chosen Zion,*
> *he has desired it for his dwelling, saying,*
> *This is my resting place forever and ever;*
> *here will I sit enthroned, for I have desired it*
> *I will bless her with abundant provisions;*
> *her poor I will satisfy with food.*
> *I will clothe her priests with salvation,*
> *and her faithful people will ever sing for joy.*
> (Ps 132:13-16)

When the two choirs met at the courtyard of the temple they burst out singing together, and all the people joined in:

> *When the Lord restored the fortunes of Zion,*
> *we were like those who were restored to health.*
> *Our mouths were filled with laughter,*

our tongues with songs of joy.
Then it was said among the nations:
"The Lord has done great things for them."
The Lord has done great things for us,
and we are filled with joy.
(Ps 126:1-3)

That day the sound of rejoicing in Jerusalem was heard throughout the land, and I raised my hands in thanksgiving to the Lord our God for supporting me until my dream had been fulfilled.

20

A BUILDER INTERVIEWS
A PROPHET

The Book of Zechariah

I, Nehemiah, had been in Jerusalem for twelve years when I made the long journey back to Susa, the capital of the Persian Empire, to report to King Artaxerxes. He renewed my appointment as governor of Judah and granted me permission to return to my beloved city. Shortly after I arrived back in Jerusalem, I inquired about the health of the elderly prophet Zechariah and was overjoyed to learn that he was still living because I wanted to visit him. The day I went to his house outside the city walls, I found him sitting on a rock under an olive tree with his hands clasped in front of him.

After I greeted him in our customary way, I told him the purpose of my visit: "Zechariah, I would like for you to share with me some of the most memorable visions and messages from the Lord that you have had during your long life here, which you would like for us to remember. Since I think it would be valuable for the people and their children to learn about these messages, I want to write them down because I am concerned that the people still have many immoral and unjust practices.

In the temple they bow and raise their hands in prayer, but outside they live just like their pagan neighbors."

"Well," he chuckled. "I can't remember what I did yesterday, but I sure can remember what the Lord commanded me to say many years ago. Let me see ... where shall I begin? Ah, yes," he said, "years ago, when I first arrived, I was appalled at the injustices. I recall the Lord saying to me, *Administer true justice, show mercy and compassion to one another. Do not oppress the widow or the fatherless, the foreigner or the poor. Do not plot evil against each other.*" (7:9,10)

His voice was weak and trembling, and I had a difficult time understanding him. I moved closer to him. He was quiet for a while. Then slowly a smile spread over his face and he said, "But even though I did condemn the evil practices, what gives me the greatest satisfaction is to recall the words of forgiveness and comfort which the Lord gave me for the people." (1:13)

"Your messages of hope helped me persist in rebuilding the walls," I said. "I remember that you had some strange and powerful visions. Please share one with me."

He shifted his weight on the rock to get more comfortable and said, "I did have some weird dreams that I felt were visions from the Lord. I remember, one night, dreaming about a man who had a measuring tape in his hand. I asked him where he was going and what he was going to do, and he told me he was going to measure Jerusalem. Then an angel appeared and said that Jerusalem was to be a city without walls because the Lord himself was going to be a wall of fire around the city. I realized that he was assuring me that the Lord would protect the city from our enemies and fill it with his glory. (2:1-5) You see, Jerusalem is the apple of his eye. (2:7) This dream gave me great comfort."

Zechariah was struggling to breathe, and I could tell it tired him to talk. He closed his eyes and dropped his head as though he was going to sleep. After a while, I wondered if I should terminate the visit and just leave. He again lifted his head, opened his eyes, and leaned back against the tree. He looked down the path on which I had come and gave me the impression he was expecting someone else.

Then he said, "But let me share with you the words I thought were most amazing. One afternoon, I had been replaying in my mind the history of our people, focusing especially on the kings that have ruled us, the wicked ones and the good ones. Out of the blue, I seemed to hear:

'Rejoice greatly, Daughter Zion!
Rejoice greatly, Daughter Jerusalem!
See your king comes to you,
righteous and victorious,
lowly and riding on a donkey,
on a colt, the foal of a donkey.
He will proclaim peace to the nations,
His rule will extend from sea to sea,
and from the Euphrates to the ends of the earth.'"
(9:9,10b)

Then he said, "I turned these words over in my mind, for some time trying to understand them, … a king riding in on a donkey… proclaiming peace…universal rule…"

I was about to interrupt him to ask who this king might be, when he continued, "Over the course of the next few months, some other strange words came to me. I don't recall the context for these: *'Strike the shepherd and the sheep will be scattered.'* (13:7)

"On another occasion, the Lord instructed me to enact an allegory in which I represent the Lord, the true shepherd of the flock, which is Israel. I break my staff, symbolizing the cancelation of the covenant with Israel due to their sins. The sheep so despise me that I reject them and demand my pay. They give me thirty pieces of silver, the value of an injured slave, and the Lord commands me to throw the silver into the treasury of the temple. (11:7-13)

"The following words troubled me, *They will look on me* (the Lord), *the one they have pierced.* (12:10b)

"And referring to prophets who will be ashamed of their ministry:

If someone asks, 'What are these wounds on your body?' they will answer, 'The wounds I was given in the house of my friends.' (13:6)

"At the time, I was not sure if these strange words could refer to the king that would be riding in on a donkey or to someone else, and even now I am not sure."

"If the last two phrases refer to the king who will ride in on a donkey," I commented, "it must mean that he will suffer."

Then I asked him, "Do you have any idea who this humble, suffering king might be?"

"As all of these words were flying around in my head," Zechariah replied, "one night, as I was walking out under the stars, the Lord gave me the following words that seemed to bring everything together. Listen to them and see if you come to the same conclusion I came to:

'I will return to Zion and dwell in Jerusalem, says the Lord. (8:3)
For I am coming, and I will live among you'.' (2:10)"

"It sounds to me like the Lord God himself will come and dwell in our midst," I said.

"That's what it sounds like to me, also," said the Zechariah.

I commented, "If this is true… what a joyous and glorious thing that will be, to have our merciful and loving God living here in Jerusalem."

"But wait," Zechariah said, "that's not all. The Lord also revealed to me that,

The Lord will be king over the whole earth.
On that day there will be one Lord,
and his name the only name".
(14:9)

"The Lord will be king not just over us, but he will reign over the whole world?" I asked.

"That's what I understand and have come to believe," he replied.

"This is mind-boggling," I said, and added, "I have trouble wrapping my mind around it… the Lord our God reigning over the whole world as a humble, suffering king! This is earthshaking."

Zechariah picked up his staff which had fallen on the ground and looking out at the distant Judean hills, he said wistfully, "Listen to these words:

This is what the Lord Almighty says: "Many peoples and the inhabitants of many cities will yet come, and the inhabitants of one city will go to another and say, 'Let us go at once and entreat the Lord and seek the Lord Almighty...' *And many peoples and powerful nations will come to Jerusalem to seek the Lord Almighty and entreat him...In those days ten people from all languages and nations will take firm hold of one Jew by the hem of his robe and say, 'Let us go with you, because we have heard that God is with you.'"* (8:20-23)

He added, "I have come to believe that the Lord God Almighty will gather peoples from every nation and ethnic group and establish his kingdom of peace and justice over the whole earth. This is the fulfillment of that part of the covenant the Lord made with our forefather Abraham when he promised,

> *"I will make you into a great nation, and I will bless you...*
> *and all peoples on earth will be blessed through you.*
> (Ge 12:2, 3)

As I walked home that afternoon, the words of another prophet, the pophet Isaiah, kept ringing in my ears. As I approached the Old Gate, also known as the Gate of Ephraim, in the northeast corner of the wall, I couldn't help but shout them out in exultant joy:

> *"In the last days*
> *the mountain of the Lord's temple will be established*
> *as the highest of the mountains;*
> *It will be exalted above the hills,*
> *and all nations will stream to it.*
> *Many peoples will come and say,*
> *'Come, let us go up to the mountain of the Lord,*
> *to the temple of the God of Jacob.*
> *He will teach us his ways,*
> *so that we may walk in his paths'*

He will judge between the nations
and will settle disputes for many peoples.
They will beat their swords into plowshares
and their spears into pruning hooks
Nation will not take up sword against nation,
nor will they train for war anymore.
(Isa 2:2-4)

Printed in the United States
By Bookmasters